SECOND EDITION

NEW PASSWORD 3
A READING AND VOCABULARY TEXT

D0817891

Linda Butler

Holyoke Community College

PEARSON
Longman

For Jim, Miles, and Clare

New Password 3 : A Reading and Vocabulary Text

Copyright © 2010 by Pearson Education, Inc.

All rights reserved.

No part of this publication may be reproduced, stored in a retrieval system, or transmitted in any form or by any means, electronic, mechanical, photocopying, recording, or otherwise, without the prior permission of the publisher.

Pearson Education, 10 Bank Street, White Plains, NY 10606

Staff credits: The people who made up the *New Password 3* team, representing editorial, production, design, and manufacturing, are: Pietro Alongi, Rhea Banker, Dave Dickey, Jaime Lieber, Maria Pia Marrella, Amy McCormick, Linda Moser, Carlos Rountree, Jennifer Stem, and Paula Van Ells.

Development editor: Thomas Ormond
Project editor: Helen B. Ambrosio
Text design & composition: ElectraGraphics, Inc.
Cover design: Maria Pia Marrella
Cover photos: iStockphoto, Ethan Vella
Illustrations: Susan Tait Porcaro, Wendy Duran

Text credits, photography credits, references, and acknowledgments appear on page xii.

Library of Congress Cataloging-in-Publication Data

Butler, Linda
New password 3 : a reading and vocabulary text / Linda Butler. — 2nd ed.
   p. cm.
Rev. ed.: Password 3 / Lynn Bonesteel, 1st. ed. 2005.
Includes bibliographical references and index.
ISBN-13: 978-0-13-246302-7 (pbk.)
ISBN-10: 0-13-246302-4 (pbk.)
ISBN-13: 978-0-13-246303-4 (pbk. with CD)
ISBN-10: 0-13-246303-2 (pbk. with CD)

1. English language—Textbooks for foreign speakers. 2. Vocabulary—Problems, exercises, etc. 3. Readers. I. Title. II. Title: New password three.
PE1128.B86139 2010
428.6'4—dc22

2009020980

PEARSON LONGMAN ON THE **WEB**

Pearsonlongman.com offers online resources for teachers and students. Access our Companion Websites, our online catalog, and our local offices around the world.

Visit us at **pearsonlongman.com**.

Printed in the United States of America

ISBN-13: 978-0-13-246302-7 2 3 4 5 6 7 8 9 10—DWL—15 14 13 12 11 10 09
ISBN-13: 978-0-13-246303-4 2 3 4 5 6 7 8 9 10—DWL—15 14 13 12 11 10 09

CONTENTS

SCOPE AND SEQUENCE

Unit/Chapter	Developing Reading Skills	Developing Other Language Skills	Target Vocabulary
UNIT 1: Let's Eat!			
Chapter 1: **Crazy about Chocolate**	• Guessing word meanings from context • Identifying the topic and main idea • Scanning • Sentences with *because*	• Discussion • Using new words • Writing a paragraph on a choice of food-related topics • Word Grammar: Nouns	*afford, average, dusty, figure out, find, get to, hide, however, let, magic, melt, professional, researcher, share, turn into*
Chapter 2: **Comfort Food**	• Scanning • Completing a graph • Identifying the main idea of a paragraph	• Discussion • Using new words • Writing a paragraph about being bored, lonely, or under stress • Word Grammar: Verbs	*bored, choice, expect, in general, lonely, mention, natural, nearly, opposite, popular, prepare, rather, specific, take part, turn out*
Chapter 3: **The Love Apple**	• Scanning • Sentences with *because* • Completing a summary	• Discussion • Using new words • Writing a paragraph about food (a choice of topics) • Word Grammar: Adjectives	*accept, area, basis, change someone's mind, come out, consider, highly, naturally, no doubt, once, root, seed, serve, tax, yet*
Chapter 4: **Slow Food**	• Scanning • Identifying the main idea of a paragraph • Completing a summary	• Role-play • Using new words • Writing a paragraph or a conversation • Word Grammar: Adjectives ending in *-ed* and *-ing*	*attack, boring, culture, danger, disappear, enemy, join, local, member, produce, reach, rush, terrible, variety, weigh*
UNIT 1 Wrap-up	• Review of the target vocabulary • Expanding Vocabulary: Nouns and verbs in word families • Building Dictionary Skills: Finding words in the dictionary (guidewords, compound words, superscripts)		
UNIT 2: Changes			
Chapter 5: **Teaching and Learning**	• What the reading does and doesn't say • Identifying the main idea of a paragraph • Writing a summary paragraph	• Role-play • Using new words • Writing a paragraph on a choice of topics • Word Grammar: Count and noncount nouns	*at all, be about to, challenge, deal with, disappointed, kind, level, memory, offer, opportunity, pick someone up, polite, quit, shock, suddenly*
Chapter 6: **"It Was Love, So Strong and So Real"**	• Stating topics of paragraphs • What the reading does and doesn't say • Making inferences	• Sharing opinions • Using new words • Writing a paragraph on a choice of topics • Word Grammar: Phrasal verbs	*alike, although, awful, comfortable, couple, difference, difficulty, discover, face, go on, marriage, no longer, responsibility, stare, total*

Unit/Chapter	Developing Reading Skills	Developing Other Language Skills	Target Vocabulary
Chapter 7: **To Live as an Artist**	• Scanning • Identifying the main idea of a paragraph • Making inferences	• Discussion • Using new words • Writing about someone you know • Word Grammar: *Hard* vs. *hardly*	*after all, against, a great deal, control, cover, energy, escape, explain, forward, get back to, hardly, lesson, manage, project, talent*
Chapter 8: **An Amazing Woman**	• What the reading does and doesn't say • Writing a summary paragraph	• Discussion • Using new words • Writing a paragraph on a choice of topics • Word Grammar: Meanings and uses of *value*	*amazing, aware, brave, bright, career, encourage, except, fear, lead, matter, notice, power, toy, value, wise*
UNIT 2 Wrap-up	• Review of the target vocabulary • Expanding Vocabulary: Nouns, verbs, and adjectives in word families • Building Dictionary Skills: Finding words in the dictionary (continued)		

UNIT 3: Starting Out in a Career

Unit/Chapter	Developing Reading Skills	Developing Other Language Skills	Target Vocabulary
Chapter 9: **A Dentist? Oh, No!**	• Scanning • Identifying and stating main ideas	• Discussion • Using new words • Writing a paragraph about making an important decision • Word Grammar: Using *suggest*	*calm, case, come up, communication, first of all, gentle, influence, lab, make up one's mind, movement, needle, relaxed, suggest, support, What do you do?*
Chapter 10: **A Cool Job**	• What the reading does and doesn't say • Defining terms • Writing a summary paragraph	• Discussion • Using new words • Writing a paragraph about your first job • Studying Collocations: Verb + noun	*by accident, certain, develop, entire, exactly, field, hardware, insect, interview, make sure, pay attention, producer, program, software, sound*
Chapter 11: **Ready for Action**	• Scanning • Defining terms • Making inferences	• Discussion • Using new words • Writing a paragraph about learning or teaching from experience • Word Grammar: Nouns as modifiers	*apply (for), as a matter of fact, available, destroy, end up, forest, leather, outdoors, patience, refer, season, sharp, tool, toward, training*
Chapter 12: **Life Is Full of Surprises**	• What the reading does and doesn't say • Defining terms • Cause and effect	• Discussion • Using new words • Writing a paragraph on a choice of topics • Studying Collocations: Adjective + preposition	*advanced, all of a sudden, cause, get into, give up, international, manage to, medical, medicine, professor, score, secure, stage, subject, work out*

THE SECOND EDITION OF THE *PASSWORD* SERIES

Welcome to *New Password*, the second edition of *Password*, a series designed to help learners of English develop their reading skills and expand their vocabularies. The series offers theme-based units consisting of

- engaging nonfiction reading passages,
- a variety of skill-development activities based on the passages, and
- exercises to help students understand, remember, and use new words.

With this new edition, the *Password* series expands from three levels to five. Each book can be used independently of the others, but when used as a series, the books will help students reach the 2,000-word vocabulary level in English, at which point, research has shown, most learners can begin to read unadapted texts.

The series is based on two central ideas. The first is that the best way for learners to develop their ability to read English is, as you might guess, to practice reading English. To spark and sustain the student's motivation to read, "second language reading instruction must find ways to avoid continually frustrating the reader."[1] Learners need satisfying reading materials at an appropriate level of difficulty, materials that do not make them feel as if they are struggling to decipher a puzzle. The level of difficulty is determined by many factors, but one key factor is the familiarity of the vocabulary. Note that

> There is now a large body of studies indicating that poor readers primarily differ from good readers in context-free word recognition, and not in deficiencies in ability to use context to form predictions.[2]

To be successful, readers must be able to recognize a great many words quickly. So in addition to providing engaging reading matter, the *New Password* series carefully controls and recycles the vocabulary.

The second idea underlying the design of the series is that textbooks should teach the vocabulary that will be most useful to learners. Corpus-based research has shown that the 2,000 highest-frequency words in English account for almost 80 percent of the running words in academic texts.[3] These are thus highly valuable words for students to learn, and these are the words targeted in the *Password* series.

The chart below shows the number of words that each *New Password* book assumes will be familiar to the learner, and the range of the high-frequency vocabulary targeted in the book.

Highest-frequency words	New Password 1	New Password 2	New Password 3	New Password 4	New Password 5
2,000					**target words** *absence, acceptable, advantage,…*
1,500				**target words** *appear, attach,…*	**words assumed** *a/an, able, about, active, address, adult, agree, almost, amount, appear, attach,…*
1,200			**target words** *active, amount,…*	**words assumed** *a/an, able, about, active, address, adult, agree, almost, amount,…*	
900		**target words** *able, adult,…*	**words assumed** *a/an, able, about, address, adult, agree, almost,…*		
600	**target words** *agree, almost,…*	**words assumed** *a/an, about, address, agree, almost,…*			
300	**words assumed** *a/an, about, address,…*				

[1]Thom Hudson, *Teaching Second Language Reading* (Oxford, UK: Oxford University Press, 2007) 291.
[2]C. Juel, quoted in *Teaching and Researching Reading*, William Grabe and Fredericka Stoller (Harlow, England: Pearson Education, 2002) 73.
[3]I. S. P. Nation, *Learning Vocabulary in Another Language* (Cambridge, England: Cambridge University Press, 2001) 17.

The vocabulary taught in the *Password* series has been carefully chosen. Target word choices are based on analyses of authentic language data in various corpora, including data in the Longman Corpus Network, to determine which words are most frequently used and most likely to be needed by the learner. Also targeted are common collocations and other multiword units, such as phrasal verbs.[4] The target vocabulary is chosen most often for its usefulness across a range of subjects but occasionally for its value in dealing with the topic of one particular chapter. Other factors in the choice of target words include the complexity of a word's meanings and uses.

While becoming a good reader in English involves much more than knowing the meanings of words, there is no doubt that vocabulary knowledge is essential. To learn new words, students need to see them repeatedly and in varied contexts. They must become skilled at guessing meaning from context but can do this successfully only when they understand the context. Research by Paul Nation and Liu Na suggests that "for successful guessing [of unknown words] . . . at least 95% of the words in the text must be familiar to the reader."[5] For that reason, the vocabulary in the readings has been carefully controlled so that unknown words should constitute no more than 5 percent of the text. The words used in a reading are limited to those high-frequency words that the learner is assumed to know plus the vocabulary targeted in the chapter and target words and phrases recycled from previous chapters. New vocabulary is explained and practiced in exercises and activities, encountered again in later chapters, and reviewed in the Unit Wrap-ups and Vocabulary Self-Tests. This emphasis on systematic vocabulary acquisition is a highlight of the *Password* series.

The second edition has expanded the series from three levels to five, increasing the number of reading passages from 76 to 104 and expanding the coverage of high-frequency vocabulary. One completely new book has joined the series, the beginning-level *New Password 1*. The other books—*New Password 2, 3, 4,* and *5*—have retained the most popular materials from the first edition of the series and added new chapters. The books vary somewhat in organization and content, to meet the diverse needs of beginning- to high-intermediate-level students, but all five feature the popular Unit Wrap-ups and the Vocabulary Self-Tests, and all five will help learners make steady progress in developing their reading, vocabulary, and other English language skills.

Linda Butler, creator of the Password *series*

Additional References

Nation, Paul. *Teaching and Learning Vocabulary*. New York: Newbury House, 1990.

Schmitt, Norbert, and Michael McCarthy, eds. *Vocabulary: Description, Acquisition, and Pedagogy*. Cambridge, UK: Cambridge University Press, 1997.

Schmitt, Norbert, and Cheryl Boyd Zimmerman. "Derivative Word Forms: What Do Learners Know?" *TESOL Quarterly* 36 (Summer 2002): 145–171.

---

[4]Dilin Liu, "The Most Frequently Used Spoken American English Idioms: A Corpus Analysis and Its Implications," *TESOL Quarterly* 37 (Winter 2003): 671–700.
[5]Nation, 254.

OVERVIEW OF *NEW PASSWORD 3*

New Password 3 is intended for students with a vocabulary of about 900 words in English, and it teaches over 300 more. Fifteen words and phrases from each nonfiction reading passage are targeted in the exercises for that chapter and recycled in later chapters. Because of the systematic building of vocabulary, as well as the progression of reading skills work, it is best to do the chapters in order.

Most of the target words are among the 1,200 highest-frequency words in English, words that students need to build a solid foundation for their language learning. Other, lower-frequency words and phrases are targeted for their usefulness in discussing a particular theme, such as *deaf, in person,* and *laughter* in Unit 5: Communication.

Organization of the Book

New Password 3 contains five units, each with four chapters followed by a Wrap-up section. Vocabulary Self-Tests are found after Units 2, 4, and 5. At the end of the book you will find the answers to the Self-Tests and an index to the target vocabulary.

THE UNITS Each unit is based on a theme and includes four chapters built around readings that deal with real people, places, events, and ideas.

THE CHAPTERS Each of the four chapters in a unit is organized as follows:

Getting Ready to Read—The chapter opens with a photo and prereading tasks. Some tasks are for pair or small-group work, others for the full class. *Getting Ready to Read* starts students thinking about the subject of the reading by drawing on what they know, eliciting their opinions, and introducing relevant vocabulary.

Reading—This section contains the reading passage for the chapter. The passages progress from about 450 to about 600 words over the course of the book, and they increase in level of reading difficulty. Students should read each passage the first time without stopping to look up or ask about new words. Let them know that the goal for this reading is getting the main ideas and that multiple readings will improve their comprehension and reading fluency. You may wish to have them reread while you read aloud or play the audio, as listening while reading can aid comprehension, retention, and pronunciation.

The reading is followed by *Quick Comprehension Check*, a brief true/false exercise to let students check their general understanding. It is a good idea to go over the *Quick Comprehension Check* statements in class: When a statement is true, ask students how they know it is true; when it is false, have students correct it. By doing so, you send them back into the reading to find support for their answers. Try to avoid spending time explaining vocabulary at this point.

Exploring Vocabulary—Once students have a general understanding of the reading, it is time to focus on new words. This section has three parts:

1. *Thinking about the Target Vocabulary*. In Chapter 1, students see the target words and phrases from the reading passage listed in a chart under *Nouns, Verbs, Adjectives,* and *Other*.* From Chapter 2 on, students are asked to find target words and phrases in the reading and write them in the correct column of the chart. Students then identify the vocabulary that is new to them and return to the reading to see what they can learn about word meanings from context. At first, students will probably benefit from working on guessing meaning from context as a whole class, with your guidance; later you may want them to discuss new word meanings in pairs. (See the Scope and Sequence on pages iv–vii for chapter-by-chapter lists of the target vocabulary.)

2. *Using the Target Vocabulary*. This section has three exercises of various types, to help students understand the meanings of the target words and phrases as they are used in the reading and in other contexts. These exercises can be done in class or out, by students working individually or in pairs.

3. *Building on the Vocabulary*. In this section, you will find either *Word Grammar*, with work on parts of speech or the meanings and uses of particular target words, or *Studying Collocations*, with information on words that go together, such as the verb + noun combinations *make a decision* and *take a chance*. (See the Scope and Sequence on pages iv–vii for the contents of *Building on the Vocabulary* sections.) After working through these materials, students can turn to their dictionaries for further information, if needed.

* In the chart, *Nouns* include noun phrases (such as *the ground*), *Verbs* include phrasal verbs (such as *figure out* and *go on*) and verb phrases (such as *change someone's mind* and *pay attention to*), *Adjectives* include participial adjectives (such as *bored* and *boring*), and *Other* includes adverbs, prepositions, etc.

Developing Your Skills—In this section are tasks that require students to delve back into the reading. They include work on recognizing and stating topics and main ideas, scanning for details, recognizing and stating cause and effect, distinguishing fact from opinion, defining terms, making inferences, and summarizing. You will also find a fluency-building exercise: *Discussion, Sharing Opinions, Role-Play,* or *Interview.* The exercise *Using New Words* has pairs of students working productively with the target vocabulary. The chapter ends with *Writing,* which offers a choice of paragraph-writing assignments. The writing exercises may be used for brief in-class writing, as prompts for journal entries, or for more formal assignments. (See the Scope and Sequence on pages iv–vii for a list of reading skills and writing assignments by chapter.)

UNIT WRAP-UP—Each unit ends with a four-part Wrap-up section that provides a key follow-up to students' initial encounters with the unit vocabulary, to consolidate and enrich their understanding of new words and phrases and to broaden their understanding of word families and dictionary use. The four parts are: *Reviewing Vocabulary, Expanding Vocabulary, A Puzzle,* and *Building Dictionary Skills,* which features excerpts from the fourth edition of the *Longman Dictionary of American English.*

The Teacher's Manual

The Teacher's Manual for *New Password 3* contains:

- The answer key for all exercises in the book
- Five unit tests with answers

- Quick Oral Reviews, sets of prompts you can use for rapid drills of vocabulary studied in each chapter. These drills can be an important part of the spaced repetition of vocabulary—repeated exposures to newly learned words and phrases at increasing intervals—that helps students remember the vocabulary. For tips on how to use the prompts, see the Introduction in the Teacher's Manual.

To the Student

Welcome to *New Password 3*! This book will help you improve your reading skills in English and expand your English vocabulary. The reading passages in it are about real people, events, ideas, and places around the world. I hope you will enjoy reading, writing, and talking about them.

About the Author

Linda Butler began her English-language teaching career in Italy in 1979. She currently teaches ESL part-time at Holyoke Community College in Holyoke, Massachusetts. She is the author of many ESL/EFL textbooks, including Books 1 through 4 of the *New Password* series and *Fundamentals of Academic Writing.*

REFERENCES, ACKNOWLEDGMENTS, AND CREDITS

REFERENCES Ackerman, J. "How to Nap," *The Boston Sunday Globe* (June 15, 2008): D10.

Cazeneuve, B. "All Chocolate, No Oompa-Loompas," *The New York Times* (December 22, 2004). Retrieved June 11, 2009, from http://www.nytimes.com/2004/12/22/dining/22CHOC_LN.html.

Cutler, K. D. "From Wolf Peach to Outer Space—Tomato History & Lore," Brooklyn Botanic Garden. Retrieved June 11, 2009, from http://www.bbg.org/gar2/topics/kitchen/handbooks/tomatoes/1.html\.

Nabhan, G. P. *Coming Home to Eat*. New York: W. W. Norton & Co., Inc., 2002.

Slow Food. http://www.slowfood.com.

ACKNOWLEDGMENTS First of all, I would like to thank the people who shared their stories with me so that students can enjoy them in this book: Mahmoud Arani, Marlin Fan, Kazumi Funamoto, Vitek Kruta, Charles Lane, Brandon Middleton, and Arunaa and Hervé Phalippou. I would also like to thank my students at Holyoke Community College (Holyoke, MA, USA) for their feedback on reading passages, in particular Julissa Garib and Lisandra Zeno, who also let me include excerpts from their journals. Many thanks as well to colleagues whose comments on the first edition of *Password 1* and *2* were much appreciated. For research assistance, I thank Jim Montgomery, Miles Montgomery-Butler, Thomas Ormond, and Beatrice Romano. I would also like to thank Lynn Bonesteel, author of *New Password 5*, for her contributions to the series.

I also very much appreciate the work of the following reviewers, who commented on early drafts of materials for the book: Simon Weedon, NOVA ICI Oita School, Japan; Joe Walther, Sookmyung Women's University, Korea; Kevin Knight, Kanda University of International Studies, Japan; Guy Elders, Turkey; Wendy Allison, Seminole Community College, Florida; Kimberly Bayer-Olthoff, Hunter College, New York; Ruth Ann Weinstein, J. E. Burke High School, Massachusetts; Vincent LoSchiavo, P.S. 163, New York; Kelly Roberts-Weibel, Edmunds Community College, Washington; Lisa Cook, Laney College, California; Thomas Leverett, Southern Illinois University, Illinois; Angela Parrino, Hunter College, New York; Adele Camus, George Mason University, Virginia.

Finally, it has been a pleasure working with Pearson Longman ELT, and for all their efforts on behalf of this book and the entire *New Password* series, I would like to thank Pietro Alongi, Editorial Director; Amy McCormick, Acquisitions Editor; Paula Van Ells, Director of Development; Thomas Ormond, Developmental Editor; Susan Tait Porcaro and Wendy Duran, Illustrators; Helen Ambrosio, Project Editor and Photo Researcher; Wendy Campbell and Carlos Rountree, Assistant Editors; and the rest of the Pearson Longman ELT team.

LB

TEXT CREDITS

Nightline: Jacques Torres, from ABCNEWS.com.

Clark, G. "Homegrown Tomatoes." Retrieved June 12, 2009, from http://www.cowboylyrics.com/lyrics/clark-guy/homegrown-tomatoes-12.html. Printed by permission of EMI Music Publishers.

PHOTOGRAPHY CREDITS p. 1, © *Shutterstock*; p. 2, © *AFP/Getty Images*; p. 13, photo by Clare Montgomery-Butler; p. 23, © *iStockphoto*; p. 33, © *Corbis/Ed Bock Photography, Inc.*; p. 49, © *Corbis/John Henley*; p. 50, Republished with permission of Globe Newspaper Company, Inc., from the April 15, 2001 issue of *The Boston Globe*, © 2001; p. 60, photo courtesy of Arunaa Phalippou; p. 70, Reprinted with permission of *The Daily Hampshire Gazette*. All rights reserved; p. 79, photo courtesy of Brown University; p. 95, © *Shutterstock*; p. 96, photo by Linda Butler; p. 106, photo courtesy Linda Butler; p. 116, © *Reuters News Media, Inc./Corbis*; p. 126, © *Brian McDonald*; p. 141, © *Dale O'Dell/Corbis*; p. 142 © *Shutterstock*; p. 152, by Ethan Vella; p. 162, by Ethan Vella; p. 172, photo of Mary Shelley © *Bettman/Corbis*; p. 189, © *Shutterstock*; p. 190, © *Royalty-Free/Corbis*; p. 201 © *Monkey Business Images/Shutterstock*; p. 211, © *Bettman/Corbis*; p. 220, photo by Ethan Vella

UNIT
1

LET'S EAT!

Crazy about Chocolate

Chef Jacques Torres

GETTING READY TO READ

Talk about these questions with a partner.

1. Which of these do you like? Check (✓) your answers, and ask your partner.

	You	Your Partner
a. chocolates[1]	☐	☐
b. chocolate bars[2]	☐	☐
c. hot chocolate	☐	☐
d. other foods with chocolate:	☐	☐

_____

[1] *chocolates*

[2] *a bar of chocolate*

2. Do you think chocolate is good for you? Tell why or why not.

3. If you are crazy about someone or something, you like that person or thing very, very much. What or who are you crazy about?

READING

Look at the picture, words, and definitions next to the reading. Then read without stopping. Don't worry about new words. Don't stop to use a dictionary. Just keep reading!

Crazy about Chocolate

1   How do you feel about chocolate? If you like it, you are far from alone. The question is, why are so many people so crazy about it?

2   Jacques Torres has always loved chocolate. When he was a child in France, his family could not **afford** to buy it very often. They used to have chocolates only at Christmas. Jacques remembers how he used to take some and go **hide** under the table, with the tablecloth[1] all around him. He did not want his mother to see how many he was eating. He says that when he bit into one of his favorites, "That was heaven!"[2]

[1] a *tablecloth*

[2] *heaven* = a place of perfect happiness

3   When he grew up, Jacques became a **professional** chef. For years, he worked at famous restaurants in France and the United States. Then he left restaurant work to start his own business. Today, he owns three chocolate shops in New York City, one with a chocolate factory next door. It feels to him like a dream come true.

4   "Everybody loves chocolate," says Jacques, "but it's such a mystery[3] to them. How does this **magic** happen?" At the factory, visitors **get to** watch it happen through 11-foot-tall windows. Jacques **lets** them see how **dusty** brown cocoa beans[4] are **turned into** beautiful chocolates.

[3] a *mystery* = something that is difficult to explain or understand

[4] *cocoa bean*s = beans from the cacao tree, used to make chocolate

5   It is clear that many people **share** Jacques' love of chocolate. His shops sell more than 300,000 pounds of it a year. **However**, no one thinks of New York City as the world capital of chocolate. That would be Switzerland, a country rich in chocolate factories. The **average** person there eats about 22 pounds of chocolate a year. Next in line after the Swiss are the chocolate-loving British. There are chocolate lovers across all of Europe, North and South America, and Australia, too. Now chocolate makers are looking to Asia for new customers.

(continued)

6   Why do people love chocolate so much? Many **researchers** have asked this question, and they have studied what chocolate does to the human brain. Scientists have **found** that chocolate has more than 300 different chemicals[5] in it. Which ones give us the good feelings we get when it **melts** in the mouth? That has been difficult to **figure out**.

7   We do now know that chocolate can be good for you. So, if you wish, you can say that you eat it for your health. Jacques Torres sees chocolate in a different way. "You know, chocolate is like romance,"[6] he says. "It makes your eyes close, your mouth water. It makes you playful." That seems a fine reason to enjoy a little chocolate.

[5] a *chemical* = a substance, especially one made by or used in chemistry

[6] *romance* = the feeling of excitement connected with love between two people

Quick Comprehension Check

Read these sentences about the reading. Circle T (true) or F (false).

1. Many people are crazy about chocolate. (T) F

2. Jacques Torres is a French chef and a lover of chocolate. T F

3. Jacques thinks most people understand how chocolate is made. T F

4. New Yorkers eat more chocolate than anyone else. T F

5. Chocolate does something to your brain when you eat it. T F

6. Jacques wants people to eat chocolate for their health. T F

EXPLORING VOCABULARY

Thinking about the Target Vocabulary

 A **The words and phrases in bold in "Crazy about Chocolate" are the target vocabulary for this chapter. They are listed in this chart in the same order as in the reading.**

- In the column on the left are the paragraph numbers.
- The next three columns are for nouns, verbs, and adjectives—three important **parts of speech**. The last column is for all other kinds of words and phrases.

	Nouns*	Verbs*	Adjectives	Other
2		afford		
		hide		
3			professional	
4	magic			
		get to		
		let		
			dusty	
		turn into		
5		share		
				however
			average	
6	researcher			
		find		
		melt		
		figure out		

* The chart shows the singular form of any plural noun from the reading. It shows the base form, or simple form, of each verb.

 B **Which words in the chart are new to you? Circle them. Then find the words in the reading. Look at the context. Can you guess the meaning?**

Guessing Meaning from Context

We use words in a **context**. The context of a word means the words and sentences before and after the word. The context can help you guess a word's meaning. For example, look at the context of *hide*:

> Jacques remembers how he used to take some and go **hide** under the table, with the tablecloth all around him. He did not want his mother to see how many he was eating.

The context of *hide* tells you that the word means "go or stay in a place where no one can see or find you."

Using the Target Vocabulary

 A These sentences are **about the reading**. Complete them with the words and phrases in the box.

✔afford	dusty	found	however	share
average	figure out	get to	professional	turns them into

1. Jacques Torres's family did not have enough money to buy chocolates very often. They could not _____afford_____ them.
2. Jacques chose cooking and baking as his life's work. He is a _____ chef.
3. People have the chance to watch chocolates being made at Jacques's factory. People _____ watch this happen.
4. The cocoa beans that Jacques uses have a dry powder on them. It is like the powder on a piece of chalk, or like the very small pieces of dirt in a house. The cocoa beans look _____.
5. Jacques takes cocoa beans, sugar, and other things and changes them into fine chocolates. He _____ chocolates.
6. Many people feel the same way about chocolate that Jacques does. They _____ his love of chocolate.

7. People buy a lot of chocolate in New York. _____, Switzerland, not New York, is the "world capital of chocolate."

8. Some Swiss eat a lot of chocolate every day. Others never eat it. The _____ person is somewhere in the middle.

9. Scientists have learned about chocolate by doing tests and other research. They have _____ that there are more than 300 chemicals in it.

10. It has not been easy for scientists to answer all their questions about chocolate. They have not been able to _____ why it makes people feel good.

B These sentences use the target words and phrases **in new contexts**. Complete them with the words and phrases in the box.

afford	dusty	found	however	share
average	figure out	get to	professional	turning it into

1. I need to clean under the bed. It's _____ under there.

2. I'd like to take a nice vacation, but I can't _____ to.

3. Researchers have _____ that the average Swiss eats about 22 pounds of chocolate a year.

4. Jan can afford to buy a car. _____, she can't afford a new one, only a used one.

5. Tomorrow is a holiday, so I'll _____ sleep late in the morning.

6. They are taking that old factory and _____ an office building.

7. We have a map, so we can _____ how to get there.

8. They'll have lots to talk about. They _____ a strong interest in sports.

9. On an _____ day, the doctor sees about twenty patients.

10. The most famous _____ magician of all time was Harry Houdini.

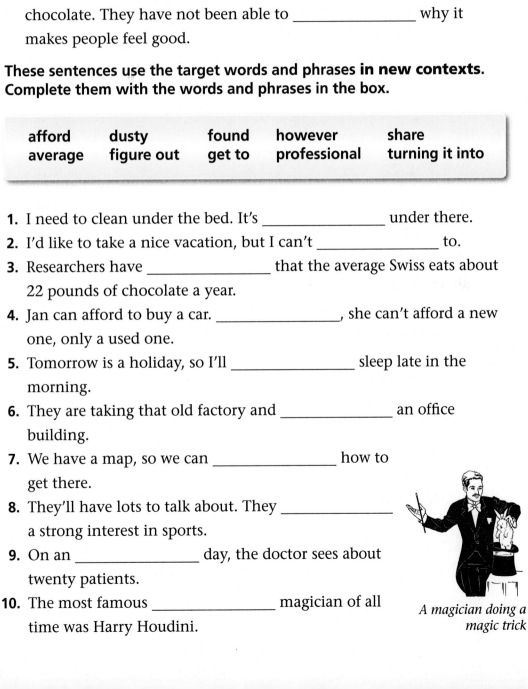

A magician doing a magic trick

Read each definition and look at the paragraph number. Look back at the reading on pages 3–4 to find the **boldfaced** word to match the definition. Copy it in the chart.

Definition	Paragraph	Target Word
1. go or stay in a place where no one can see or find you	2	hide
2. something you cannot explain, that someone makes happen in a secret way	4	
3. allows or permits someone to do something	4	
4. people who study a subject to find new facts about it	6	
5. changes from a solid to a liquid (like ice to water) because of heat	6	

Building on the Vocabulary: Word Grammar

Nouns are words for

people: *student, Eliza, boy*

places: *airport, Mexico, home*

things: *book, Honda, apple*

ideas: *education, hope, information*

Some nouns are written as two words (*hot dog, New York*). Most nouns can be **singular** (only one: *a friend, the door*) or **plural** (more than one: *two friends, the doors*).

A **proper noun** starts with a capital letter and names one special person (*Jacques*), place (*the Pacific Ocean*), or thing (*Volkswagen*).

Most nouns are **common nouns** and do not start with a capital letter (*man, ocean, car*).

There are two nouns in each sentence. Circle the nouns.

1. They are going to (Madrid) by (train).

2. The researchers at the hospital will figure it out.

3. Cats and dust make me sneeze. Ah *CHOO*!

4. The children are hiding behind the tree.

5. You and Tom can share the cookies.

6. The chocolate melted in my hand.

7. What is Dr. King's profession?

8. Your idea worked like magic.

DEVELOPING YOUR SKILLS

The Topic and the Main Idea

Answer the questions about the topic and the main idea of the reading.

> A reading has a **topic**. Ask, "What is the reading about?" The answer is the topic.

1. What is the topic of the reading? Check (✓) your answer.
   - ☐ **a.** crazy people
   - ☐ **b.** chocolate lovers
   - ☐ **c.** reasons why we eat chocolate

> A reading has a **main idea**. Ask, "What does the reading say about the topic?" The answer is the main idea.

2. What is the main idea of the reading? Check (✓) your answer.
   - ☐ **a.** Chocolate goes to the brain and makes people do crazy things.
   - ☐ **b.** Jacques Torres shares a love of chocolate with people all over the world.
   - ☐ **c.** People eat chocolate because it is a health food that makes us feel good.

Scanning

> Sometimes you need to find a piece of information in a reading. To
> do this, you **scan** the reading. *Scan* means to read very quickly and
> look for just the information you need.

**Read these statements about "Crazy about Chocolate." Scan the
reading for the information you need to complete them.**

1. Jacques Torres grew up in _____.
2. He grew up to be a professional _____.
3. Now he owns _____ chocolate shops in

   _____.

4. Visitors to his _____ can watch chocolates being made.
5. His shops sell _____ a year.
6. _____ is the world capital of chocolate.
7. The average Swiss eats _____ of chocolate a year.
8. After the Swiss, the people who eat the most chocolate are

   _____.

9. There are _____ different chemicals in chocolate.
10. Researchers have studied what the chemicals in chocolate do to the
    human _____.

Sentences with *Because*

> Sentences with *because* answer the question *Why*? The sentences
> have two parts. The part that starts with *because* can come first or
> second in the sentence.
>
> *Jacques didn't eat chocolates often **because his family couldn't
> afford them**.*
>
> ***Because his family couldn't afford chocolates**, Jacques didn't eat
> them often.*

A **Complete the sentences. Use information from the reading.**

1. Jacques hid under the table because _____

_____.

2. Jacques left restaurant work because _____

_____.

3. Switzerland is "the world capital of chocolate" because _____

_____.

4. Researchers have studied chocolate because _____

_____.

B **Circle _would_ or _wouldn't_. Complete the sentence.**

I (would / wouldn't) like to own a chocolate factory because _____

_____.

Discussion

Talk about these questions in a small group or with the whole class.

1. What do you know about Jacques Torres? Tell what you remember about him from the reading.

2. Do people in your country eat a lot of chocolate? How and when do people eat it?

3. Jacques Torres says his shops and chocolate factory are like a dream come true. What did you dream about as a child?

Using New Words

Work with a partner. Choose five target words or phrases from the chart on page 5. On a piece of paper, use each word or phrase in a sentence. (Do not choose the easiest ones! This is a chance to learn more about words or phrases you do not understand well.)

Examples:

I always wanted a pet when I was growing up, but I never <u>got to</u> have one.

Water <u>turns into</u> ice when you put it in the freezer.

My friend <u>lets</u> me drive his car.

The library is a good place to study. <u>However</u>, it closes too early.

I have <u>found</u> that it is not a good idea to lend money to my roommate.

Writing

Choose idea 1, 2, or 3 and write a short paragraph about it.

1. Write about a food that you think is good for people's health. (What is it good for? Who says that it is good? Do you eat it?) If you wish, you can begin: Eating . . . is good for people's health.

2. Write about a food that you like to make. (How do you make it? When do you eat it?) If you wish, you can begin: I like to make . . .

3. Describe a food from your country. (What is it like? Do you eat it often or only at special times?) If you wish, you can begin: I come from . . . , and many people in my country love . . .

Example:

Idea 1

Apples

Apples are good for people's health. My mother always said, "A diario una manzana es cosa sana." It is the same idea as "An apple a day keeps the doctor away." Most kinds of fruit are good for you. They have vitamins and other things I don't know about, but I know they are good for you. I eat an apple a day and other kinds of fruit, too.

CHAPTER 2

Comfort Food

"One man's comfort food"

GETTING READY TO READ

Answer these questions. Then talk about your answers with a partner or in a small group.

1. Imagine that it's late at night. You are tired, but you have to study. You are hungry, too. What would you choose to eat? Name three things.

   _____   _____   _____

2. Are these statements true or false? Circle your answers.

   a. I miss food from home.   True   False

   b. People eat when they feel sad.   True   False

   c. People eat when they feel nervous.   True   False

   d. People eat when they want to celebrate.   True   False

Look at the pictures, words, and definitions next to the reading. Then read without stopping. Don't worry about new words. Don't stop to use a dictionary. Just keep reading!

Comfort Food

1   It is **natural** for people to eat when they are hungry, but people eat for other reasons, too. Do you ever eat because you are with friends and everyone else is eating? Do you ever eat because you feel tired, or because you are under stress? Many people do. Maybe they have too much to do, or they feel nervous. Maybe they are having problems in a relationship. So they eat to feel better. But they do not eat just anything. They want a **specific** kind of food. They want food that helps them relax. They want comfort food.

2   What is comfort food? For most people, it is food that is easy to **prepare** and easy to eat. Eating it gives them a warm feeling. It is often a type of food that they loved as children. Maybe they used to eat it at specific times or places. Maybe it is food their mother used to make. Comfort food makes people feel, "Somebody's taking care of me."

3   Researchers at the University of Illinois did a survey[1] on comfort food in the United States. They asked over 1,000 people about it. They wanted to know two things: What comfort foods did people want, and when did they want them? The results of the survey were **rather** surprising.

4   The researchers **expected** people's favorite comfort food to be soft and warm, like, for example, the most **popular** comfort foods in Japan, miso soup and soba noodles.[2] But the number one U.S. comfort food was not soft or warm. It **turned out** to be potato chips. Another favorite was ice cream, especially among people ages 18 to 34. Not all comfort foods are snack foods,[3] however. **Nearly** half of the comfort foods that people described were healthy, homemade foods, such as chicken soup and mashed potatoes.[4]

5   The survey showed that people of different ages want different comfort foods. It also showed that men and women

[1] a *survey* = a set of questions you ask a large group of people to learn their opinions

[2] *Soba noodles* are made from buckwheat.

[3] *snack foods* = kinds of food that people buy ready-made to eat between meals

[4] *mashed potatoes*

make different **choices**. **In general**, women choose sweet comfort foods. Those who **took part** in the survey **mentioned** ice cream most often (74% of them put it on their list), then chocolate (69%), and cookies (66%). Ice cream was very popular with the men, too: 77% of the men in the survey mentioned it. However, men do not choose sweet foods as often as women do. Men often want hot and salty comfort foods such as soup (73%) and pizza or pasta (72%).

6   The researchers also figured out when the people in the study wanted comfort food most. You may think that comfort food is usually for times of stress, or when someone feels **bored** or **lonely**. However, the researchers say that the **opposite** is true. Yes, people do eat to feel better, but more often, they eat comfort foods when they already feel happy. They eat them to celebrate or to reward themselves.[5]

[5] *reward themselves = give themselves something nice because they did a good thing*

Quick Comprehension Check

Read these sentences about the reading. Circle T (true) or F (false).

1. People eat for a number of different reasons.   T   F

2. Comfort food is food that makes you feel good.   T   F

3. The researchers did a study of all kinds of food.   T   F

4. The top comfort food in the United States is potato chips.   T   F

5. Men and women agree about the best comfort foods.   T   F

6. People want comfort food most when they feel sad.   T   F

EXPLORING VOCABULARY

Thinking about the Target Vocabulary

 A Find the two nouns in **bold** in "Comfort Food." Add them to the chart. Write them in the order they appear in the reading. Use the singular form of any plural noun.

	Nouns	Verbs	Adjectives	Other
1			natural	
			specific	
2		prepare		
3				rather
4		expect		
			popular	
		turn out		
				nearly
5				
				in general
		take part		
		mention		
6			bored	
			lonely	

B Which words are new to you? Circle them in the chart. Then find the words in the reading. Look at the context. Can you guess the meaning?

Using the Target Vocabulary

A These sentences are **about the reading**. What is the meaning of each **boldfaced** word? Circle a, b, or c.

1. People eat when they are hungry. That's the **natural** thing to do. In this sentence, *natural* means
   a. crazy, stupid.   **b.** normal, usual.   **c.** strange, surprising.

2. Sometimes we get hungry for a **specific** kind of food—comfort food. A specific kind is
   a. one kind and no other.
   b. any kind we can get.
   c. every kind there is.

3. Comfort food doesn't usually take a lot of work. It's easy to **prepare**. *Prepare* means
   a. melt.
   b. turn into.
   c. get ready.

4. The information from the survey was **rather** surprising. *Rather* means
   a. more than a little
   b. not at all.
   c. of course.

5. The researchers **expected** the top comfort food to be warm and soft. When you expect something, you
   a. can afford it.
   b. think it will happen.
   c. share it.

6. Many of the comfort foods people talked about were snack foods, but **nearly** half of the foods were not. *Nearly* means
   a. completely.
   b. almost.
   c. ever.

7. Men and women often make different **choices** in comfort food. *Their choices* means the things that they
   a. figure out.
   b. throw.
   c. choose.

8. Many women in the survey **mentioned** ice cream. If you mention something, you
   a. say a few words about it.
   b. get to do it.
   c. do research on it.

9. Some people eat comfort food when they are **lonely**. It makes them feel less alone. *Lonely* means
   a. tired of being with people.
   b. away from friends and feeling sad.
   c. happy and relaxed.

10. Some people eat when they feel **bored**. It gives them something to do. *Bored* means
    a. tired of having nothing fun to do.
    b. very busy.
    c. ready to go to work.

B These sentences use the target words **in new contexts**. Complete them with the words in the box.

bored	expect	mention	nearly	rather
choice	lonely	natural	prepared	specific

1. They _____ a wonderful meal for their guests.

2. Jane talked about the book she's reading, but she didn't _____ the name of it.

3. The students almost went to sleep in class. They were very _____.

4. Let's call Dave and see if he's OK. He has no family, so he gets _____ on holidays.

5. Which movie would you like to see? My first _____ would be *Dark of the Night*.

6. This is Miki's first trip away from home. It's _____ that she misses her family.

7. The party was a complete surprise to Dan. He didn't _____ it.

8. I don't have any _____ plans for the weekend. I just want to relax.

9. This box is _____ heavy. Can you help me with it?

10. I washed the clothes and put them in the dryer. They should be _____ dry now.

C Read these sentences. Match the **boldfaced** target words and phrases with their definitions.

a. I thought my team would win, but it didn't **turn out** that way.

b. **In general**, his parents don't let him stay out after midnight.

c. There are lots of things happening after school that students can **take part** in.

d. Chocolate is very **popular** in Switzerland.

e. The **opposite** of *popular* is *unpopular*.

Target Words and Phrases	Definitions

1. _____popular_____ = liked by many people

2. _____ = happen or end in a specific way, have a specific result

3. _____ = usually, in most situations

4. _____ = be active in a sport, club, or other event with other people

5. _____ = a person or thing that is as different as can be from someone or something else

Building on the Vocabulary: Word Grammar

Every sentence needs a **verb**. Most verbs are words for actions. For example, *run*, *fly*, *dance*, and *play* are verbs. The words *have*, *know*, and *be* are also verbs. They are nonaction verbs.

A verb can have more than one part: *can dance*, *has been working*, and *don't talk*, for example.

The base form of some verbs has more than one word, like *figure out* and *turn into*. These are **phrasal verbs**. (See page 66 for more information.)

Circle the verb in each sentence. Remember: A verb can be more than one word.

1. He (is) a professional magician.

2. (Don't mention) it.

3. First, melt the butter.

4. He is hiding the candy from the children.

5. I'm lonely.

6. Please share this with your brother.

7. They can't afford it.

8. Everything turned out fine in the end.

DEVELOPING YOUR SKILLS

Scanning

Read these questions about "Comfort Food." Scan the reading and write the answers.

1. Why do people eat? Give three or more reasons. _____

   _____

   _____

2. What is "comfort food"? Complete this definition with quotations from the second paragraph. (Use those same words.)

   Comfort food is food that helps people relax. It's "easy to

   ___prepare___ and _____." Eating comfort food gives
      (a)   (b)

   "a _____ feeling," and it "makes people feel 'Somebody's
          (c)

   _____.'"
           (d)

3. What were the researchers' two main questions?

   a. _____

   b. _____

4. Who thinks of miso soup and soba noodles as comfort foods?

   _____

5. What is the number one comfort food for people in the United

   States? _____

6. Who especially likes ice cream? _____

7. What are two examples of healthy, homemade comfort foods?

   _____

8. How are men's and women's comfort food choices different? _____

   _____

Focusing on Details

Complete the information about U.S. men in the graph on page 21. Write the kinds of food and the percentage of men who mentioned it. Then draw a similar graph for U.S. women.

Survey Results

Main Ideas

What is the main idea of paragraph 6 in the reading? Check (✓) your answer.

☐ **1.** Stress makes people want to eat comfort foods.

☐ **2.** People want comfort food most when they are already feeling good.

☐ **3.** The researchers wanted to know when people usually eat.

Discussion

Talk about these questions in a small group. Then tell the class the results of your discussion.

1. List five comfort foods that people mentioned in the survey. Do people in your group like them? Make a chart.

Common U.S. Comfort Foods	Number of People Who Like It	Number Who Don't Like It	Total Number in the Group
1.			
2.			
3.			
4.			
5.			

2. Can you give the numbers from your group as percentages? For example: *Fifty percent (50%) of the people in our group like ice cream.*

You can also say, " ___Three___ out of ___six___ people
　　　　　　　　　(number)　　　　　　　　(total)
in our group like ___ice cream___."
　　　　　　　　　(food)

3. What do you think are the favorite comfort foods in your country?

Using New Words

Work with a partner. Choose five target words or phrases from the chart on page 16. On a piece of paper, use each word or phrase in a sentence. (Remember: Do not choose the easiest ones! This is a chance to learn more about words or phrases you do not understand well.)

Examples:

I wanted to see a movie last weekend, so I <u>mentioned</u> the idea to my friends.

The movie <u>turned out</u> to be bad, so everybody was mad at me.

I didn't <u>expect</u> my classmates to sing "Happy Birthday" to me.

"Awake" is the <u>opposite</u> of "asleep."

I am not <u>taking part</u> in any clubs or sports teams.

Writing

When do you feel bored, lonely, or under stress? What do you do? Choose one of these topics and write a paragraph of six or more sentences.

Example:

When I feel lonely, I call a friend or someone in my family. Talking usually helps me feel better. Sometimes nobody answers the phone, and then I feel bad, but I leave messages for them. I try not to stay in my room by myself. I take my homework and go someplace where there are other people. Maybe I will talk to somebody, or maybe not. But I think it is a better way to pass the time when I feel lonely.

CHAPTER 3

The Love Apple

Beautiful and delicious

GETTING READY TO READ

Talk with a partner or in a small group.

1. What are tomatoes?

   a. vegetables   **c.** berries

   b. fruit   **d.** all of the above

2. People use tomatoes to prepare many different dishes. How many can you name? Make a list.

   _____   _____

   _____   _____

   _____   _____

   _____   _____

   _____   _____

READING

Look at the words and definitions next to the reading. Then read without stopping. Don't worry about new words. Don't stop to use a dictionary. Just keep reading!

The Love Apple

1   Ah, the tomato, so well-loved by foodies[1] everywhere! The French used to call it *la pomme d'amour*, "the love apple." Today, cooks around the world work their magic with it. There are more than 4,000 types of tomatoes and **no doubt** even more ways to eat them. Without the tomato, we would have no Mexican salsa or Italian pizza. Many wonderful Indian dishes would not be the same. After the potato, it is the most popular vegetable in the world. But wait—is it a vegetable?

2   You may be thinking, "Who cares?" But this question **once** came before[2] the highest court in the United States. It happened back in 1893. At that time, there was a **tax** on vegetables brought into the country but no tax on imported[3] fruit. **Naturally**, importers of tomatoes called them fruit so as not to pay the tax. Not everyone agreed, and the question went all the way to the Supreme Court. The justices[4] knew that the tomato really is a fruit. That is because it is the part of the plant holding the **seeds**. To be more specific, it is a berry. However, most people **considered** it a vegetable. They usually cooked and ate tomatoes more like vegetables than like fruit. That was the **basis** for the Court's decision. The justices said the tomato should be called— and taxed as—a vegetable.

3   The story of the tomato really begins much earlier. It starts in South America, where tomatoes grew wild. The first people to grow them were the Mayans. In the 1500s, the Spanish took tomatoes from Mexico to Spain. From there, tomatoes went to France, Italy, and other **areas** around the Mediterranean Sea. Those first tomatoes were small and yellow. Their color gave the tomato its Italian name, *pomodoro*, or *pomo d'oro*, "golden apple."

4   Europeans did not fall in love with tomatoes quickly. For a long time, they were afraid to eat them. The tomato plant looks like a plant called deadly nightshade, or belladonna, and

[1] a *foodie* = (informal) a person who knows about and enjoys good food

[2] *came before* = had to be decided by (someone important)

[3] *imported* = brought into a country to sell

[4] *justices* = judges

is part of the same family. The **roots**, leaves, and berries of the deadly nightshade are **highly** poisonous.[5] So it took a while for Europeans to **accept** the tomato. The first cookbook with tomato recipes[6] did not **come out** until 1692.

5   By the late 1700s, Europeans were happily eating tomatoes. However, in the United States, most people did not **yet** trust them. President Thomas Jefferson (1743–1826) helped to **change their minds**. He grew tomatoes in his gardens and **served** them at dinners in the White House. Today, 85 percent of U.S. home gardeners grow tomatoes. They would no doubt agree with the words of this song:

> *Only two things that money can't buy*
>
> *That's true love and homegrown tomatoes*
>
>   —from "Homegrown Tomatoes" by Guy Clark

[5] *poisonous* = very dangerous to eat or drink

[6] a *recipe* = a set of instructions for cooking something

Quick Comprehension Check

Read these sentences about the reading. Circle T (true) or F (false).

1. Cooks use tomatoes in many different parts of the world.   T   F

2. The tomato is a kind of fruit.   T   F

3. Tomatoes were called vegetables by U.S. law.   T   F

4. The first tomatoes grew in Italy.   T   F

5. The tomato plant looks like a plant that can kill you.   T   F

6. A U.S. president introduced tomatoes to Europeans.   T   F

EXPLORING VOCABULARY

Thinking about the Target Vocabulary

 Find the five verbs in **bold** in "The Love Apple." Add them to the chart. Write them in the order they appear in the reading. Use the base form of each verb.

	Nouns	Verbs	Adjectives	Other
1				no doubt
2				once
	tax			
				naturally
	seed			
	basis			
3	area			
4	root			
				highly
5				yet
		*		

* *Change someone's mind* is a verb phrase.

 Which words are new to you? Circle them in the chart. Then find the words in the reading. Look at the context. Can you guess the meaning?

Using the Target Vocabulary

 These sentences are about the reading. Complete them with the words and phrases in the box.

accept	came out	consider	no doubt	served
basis	change their minds	highly	once	yet

1. There are more than 4,000 types of tomatoes. _____ there are even more ways to eat them. We can be sure that this is true.

2. The U.S. Supreme Court _____ had to decide the question, "Is the tomato a vegetable or a fruit?" This happened at some time in the past.

3. Most people in the United States think of the tomato as a vegetable. They don't _____ it a fruit.

4. The Supreme Court justices looked at the way most U.S. cooks used tomatoes. That was the _____ of their decision. They used that as the reason for their decision.

5. The fruit of the deadly nightshade is very dangerous. It is _____ poisonous.

6. Europeans at first did not believe that tomatoes were good to eat. It took a long time for them to _____ this idea.

7. The first cookbook that mentioned tomatoes as good to eat _____ in 1692. People could first buy it in 1692.

8. By the end of the 1700s, most Europeans were eating tomatoes, but people in the United States were not eating them _____. They would eat them later, but it had not happened at that time.

9. In the late 1700s, most people in the United States did not trust the tomato. President Thomas Jefferson helped to _____. They started to see tomatoes differently.

10. Jefferson _____ tomatoes at White House dinners. He had dishes made with tomatoes brought to the table for his guests.

B These sentences use the target words and phrases **in new contexts.** Complete them with the words and phrases in the box.

accept	changed my mind	consider	no doubt	serve
basis	come out	highly	once	yet

1. I _____ her one of my best friends.

2. We haven't seen Roberto _____, but he should be here soon.

3. That new movie is going to _____ next weekend.

4. He doesn't want to see her anymore. I know it hurts, but she'll have to _____ it.

5. Be careful! It says "_____ flammable." That means it can catch fire very easily.

6. Let's call her. It's ten o'clock, so _____ she's awake by now.

7. It's a vegetarian restaurant. That means they don't _____ meat.

8. I used to think chocolate was bad for you, but I've _____.

9. The idea that tomatoes were dangerous to eat had no _____ in fact.

10. I _____ expected them to get married, but I don't anymore.

C Read these sentences. Match the **boldfaced** target words with their definitions.

a. Can they move that tree, or are the **roots** too deep?

b. When I cook with tomatoes, I don't use the **seeds**.

c. The team lost the big game, so **naturally**, they all feel bad.

d. You have to add the 5 percent sales **tax** to the price.

e. My family couldn't afford a house in that **area**.

Target Words	Definitions

1. _____ = in a way that you would expect

2. _____ = a part of a place, city, country, etc.[1]

3. _____ = small hard objects produced by plants, from which a new plant can grow

4. _____ = the parts of a plant or tree that grow under the ground

5. _____ = money you have to pay to the government based on what you buy, how much money you make, where you live, etc.

[1] *Etc.* is short for the Latin phrase *et cetera*. This abbreviation is often used at the end of a list. It means "and other people or things of the same kind."

Building on the Vocabulary: Word Grammar

An **adjective** is a word that describes

a person:	a *popular* boy, *fast* runners
a place:	*beautiful* cities, a *large* airport
a thing:	a *tall* building, *small* cars
an idea:	*new* information, a *nice* surprise

An adjective can come before a noun: *I have **good friends**.*

An adjective can follow the verb *be*, *get*, or *feel*: *Mary and John **are happy**. Please **get ready**. I feel **tired**.*

Adjectives have no plural form.

Circle the adjective in each sentence.

1. It's not (expensive).

2. My computer gets dusty.

3. It was just an average day.

4. She is a professional basketball player.

5. Do you think he's lonely?

6. I have a specific color in mind.

7. It is natural for babies to cry sometimes.

8. What do you do when you feel bored?

DEVELOPING YOUR SKILLS

Scanning

Read these questions about "The Love Apple." Scan the reading and write short answers.

1. Who called the tomato "the love apple"? _____
2. What are three examples of countries where tomatoes are an important food? _____
3. In what year did the U.S. Supreme Court make its tomato decision?

   _____
4. Where did the first wild tomatoes grow? _____
5. Where did people first plant them? _____
6. What is deadly nightshade? _____
7. When did the first cookbook with tomato recipes come out?

   _____
8. Who was Thomas Jefferson? _____

Sentences with *Because*

Complete the sentences. Use information from the reading.

1. The tomato is a fruit because _____

   _____.
2. The U.S. Supreme Court called the tomato a vegetable because

   _____.
3. Many people thought it was dangerous to eat tomatoes because

   _____.
4. Thomas Jefferson was important in the history of the tomato because

   _____.

Summarizing

> A **summary** is a short report on a longer reading. It has only the main information.

Complete this summary of the reading. You will need to write more than one word in some of the blanks.

The tomato is a _____, but many people consider it a
(1)

_____. It is the second most _____
(2)   (3)

in _____. Tomatoes first grew in _____
(4)   (5)

and later became popular in _____.
(6)

People in Europe and the United States did not accept them at first

because _____.
(7)

Discussion

Talk about these questions in a small group or with the whole class.

1. What facts do you remember about the history of the tomato? Tell as much as you can about it.

2. How important are tomatoes to people in your country? Why?

3. What foods can you name that are popular with some people but that others are afraid to eat? Do you eat any of these foods?

Using New Words

Work with a partner. Choose five target words or phrases from the chart on page 26. On a piece of paper, use each word or phrase in a sentence. (Remember: Do not choose the easiest ones! This is a chance to learn more about words or phrases you do not understand well.)
Examples:
My friends and I were always happy when a new Harry Potter movie _came out._

I _consider_ myself a lucky person.

My hometown _once_ had many farms, but now it is all city.

Writing

Choose a topic and write a paragraph about it. Write six sentences or more.

1. People often have foods that they think they could not live without. What favorite food do you feel that strongly about? Why is it so important to you? If you wish, you can begin: I could not live without . . .

2. Is there a food that others like but you would never eat? Explain how you feel about this food and why. If you wish, you can begin: Some people consider . . . good to eat, but I do not.

CHAPTER 4

Slow Food

A traditional meal to enjoy

GETTING READY TO READ

Talk with your whole class.

1. What is fast food? Write a definition: Fast food is food that _____
_____.

2. How many examples of fast food can you think of? Make a list.

3. Fill in this chart.

What's good about fast food?	What's bad about fast food?

4. What do you think the phrase *slow food* means?

READING

Look at the pictures, words, and definitions next to the reading. Then read without stopping. Don't worry about new words. Don't stop to use a dictionary. Just keep reading!

Slow Food

1   Italians know and love good food. It is at the heart of their **culture**. So is taking the time to enjoy their food. They do not like to **rush** through meals. As a result, many of them think that fast food is a **terrible** idea.

2   In 1986, the first American fast-food restaurant—a McDonald's—opened in Rome. Many Italians were surprised and angry. They thought of it as an **attack** on Italian culture. One man, Carlo Petrini, decided to fight back. "Fast food is the **enemy**," he said, and he started a group called Slow Food. Today, over 85,000 people in 132 countries belong to the group. More people **join** every day.

3   The **members** of Slow Food share many of the same ideas. They believe that there are many problems with food today. Fast food is one of them. They consider fast food a problem because it is not healthy food and because it is the same everywhere. That is **boring**, they say. They want to keep traditional cooking with all its wonderful **variety**.

4   Slow Food members worry about a second problem, too. Some types of plants and animals are becoming very rare,[1] and the world is in **danger** of losing them completely. Some examples are

- A kind of fava bean grown only on the Greek island of Santorini
- Several kinds of dates[2] grown only in the area around Siwa, Egypt
- The blue-egg chickens of Temuco, Chile
- The pirarucù, a fish that lives in the Amazon River and can **weigh** more than 500 pounds (as much as 250 kilograms)

[1] *rare* = uncommon and hard to find

[2] *dates*

Slow Food does not want to let these plants and animals **disappear**, so the organization[3] is working with **local** groups to stop that from happening.

5   There is a third problem that worries Slow Food members. Much of our food today is **produced** by big companies. These companies sell their products in distant places, so they want products that can travel well. Big growers[4] want the kinds of fruit and vegetables that look good after a long trip. But how do their apples and lettuce and tomatoes taste? That is less important to them. So now we have more trouble finding good-tasting food.

6   Today, it has become common to eat foods from far away. Foods eaten in the United States travel an average of 1,300 miles to **reach** the dinner table. In the past, people got most of their food from farms and factories in their local area. Slow Food members say, "People should be buying more local food. It's fresh, and it's part of our culture." One man in the United States, Gary Nabhan, decided to try this. For one year, all his food came from plants and animals near his home in Arizona. One local animal is the rattlesnake.[5] Nabhan ate that, too! In his book *Coming Home to Eat*, he says it tastes just like chicken.

7   Fast food is reaching more and more parts of the world. But Slow Food is getting its message to more and more people, too.

[3] an *organization* = a group, such as a club or business, formed for a specific reason

[4] *big growers* = large farm companies

[5] a *rattlesnake*

Quick Comprehension Check

Read these sentences about the reading. Circle T (true) or F (false).

1. Good food is an important part of life in Italy.   T   F

2. The group Slow Food opened a McDonald's in Rome.   T   F

3. Slow Food members say fast food is not interesting or healthy.   T   F

4. Slow Food members want everyone to eat
   Italian food.   T   F

5. They say there are too many types of food in
   the world.   T   F

6. Big food producers sell their products in faraway
   places.   T   F

EXPLORING VOCABULARY

Thinking about the Target Vocabulary

 A Find the three adjectives in **bold** in "Slow Food." Add them to the chart. Write them in the order they appear in the reading.

	Nouns	Verbs	Adjectives	Other
1	culture			
		rush		
2	attack			
	enemy			
		join		
3	member			
	variety			
4	danger			
		weigh		
		disappear		
5		produce		
6		reach		

B Which words are new to you? Circle them in the chart. Then find the words in the reading. Look at the context. Can you guess the meaning?

Using the Target Vocabulary

 These sentences are about the reading. Complete them with the words in the box.

boring	join	produce	rush	weigh
disappear	local	reach	variety	

1. Italians don't want to hurry at mealtime. They don't like to
   _____ through meals.
2. The group Slow Food is growing. More people _____ it
   every day.
3. If food becomes the same everywhere, it will be less interesting. It
   will be _____ .
4. The group Slow Food wants there to be many different types of food.
   They want _____ in food.
5. The pirarucù can grow very big and get very heavy. It can
   _____ over 500 pounds.
6. There are now very few of some kinds of plants and animals. They
   may go away completely. Slow Food doesn't want these plants and
   animals to _____ .
7. Slow Food works with groups of people near the places where rare
   plants and animals live. Those are _____ groups.
8. People used to grow their own food. Now big companies
   _____ most of our food.
9. Food often travels far before it gets to our homes. It may travel many
   miles to _____ your dinner table.

These sentences use the target words **in new contexts**. Complete them with the words in the box.

boring	joined	produces	rushing	weighed
disappeared	local	reach	variety	

1. The baby _____ nine pounds when he was born.

2. The newspaper gives both the national weather and our _____ weather.

3. The plane will be taking off on time, so we should _____ Tokyo on time.

4. Farmers in California grow a wide _____ of vegetables.

5. Don't worry, we have lots of time. Stop _____ around and relax a little!

6. What a _____ movie! It almost put me to sleep.

7. Tomas _____ an athletic club. Now he goes there to exercise.

8. We all went to the party together, but then he _____ and we didn't see him again.

9. Argentina _____ a lot of meat, wheat, and corn.

C Read each definition and look at the paragraph number. Look back at the reading on pages 34–35 to find the **boldfaced** word to match the definition. Copy it in the chart.

Definition	Paragraph	Target Word
1. the ideas, beliefs, art, and behavior of a specific society or group of people	1	
2. very, very bad	1	
3. a violent act to try to hurt someone or something	2	
4. someone you are fighting in a war; the opposite of *friend*	2	
5. people who belong to a group, club, or organization	3	
6. the chance that someone or something will be hurt	4	

Building on the Vocabulary: Word Grammar

There are many pairs of adjectives that end in *-ing* and *-ed*.
- The *-ed* adjective usually describes a person. It tells how someone feels: *I'm **surprised** to see you here!*
- The *-ing* adjective describes the thing that causes the feeling: *They told us some **surprising** news.*
- The *-ing* adjective can also describe a person: *He's a **boring** speaker.*

A **Complete the sentences. Use each adjective only once.**

1. (surprising, surprised) It was _____ news. Everyone was
(a)
_____.
(b)

2. (boring, bored) What a _____ class! I was completely
(a)
_____.
(b)

3. (interesting, interested) He's _____ in magic. Magic is
(a)
very _____ to him.
(b)

4. (exciting, excited) I'm _____ about my vacation. It's
(a)
going to be _____.
(b)

5. (tiring, tired) I'm _____. Today was a _____
(a)   (b)
day.

B **Write four sentences. Use *-ed* and *-ing* adjectives.**

1. _____

2. _____

3. _____

4. _____

DEVELOPING YOUR SKILLS

Scanning

Read the questions below. Then go back to the reading and scan it for the answers.

1. How do Italians feel about good food? _____

_____

2. What happened in Rome in 1986? _____

3. Who is Carlo Petrini? _____

4. What three problems worry the members of Slow Food?

a. _____

b. _____

c. _____

5. Why don't some fruits and vegetables taste good? _____

_____

6. How far does food travel (on average) in the United States?

_____

7. What do Slow Food members think about local food? _____

_____

8. What did Gary Nabhan do? _____

_____

Main Ideas

What is the main idea of paragraph 2 in the reading? Check (✓) your answer.

☐ **1.** In 1986, a McDonald's restaurant opened in Rome, Italy.

☐ **2.** Fast-food restaurants have become more and more popular in Italy.

☐ **3.** The group Slow Food began as a way to fight back against fast-food restaurants.

Summarizing

Complete this summary of the reading.

Slow Food is a group with members in 132 countries. It started because

_____.

Slow Food members care about _____.

They want people to _____.

Role-Play

Form a small group. One or two of you are members of Slow Food. One or two of you are reporters for a newspaper or TV program, and you eat fast food every day. The reporters ask questions. For example, they can ask the Slow Food members about their group, their ideas about food, and what they eat. The Slow Food members answer the questions and also ask the reporters questions of their own.

Using New Words

Work with a partner. Choose five target words from the chart on page 36. On a piece of paper, use each word in a sentence.
Examples:
I rushed to get to class this morning.
When you play some sports, you are in danger of getting hurt.
Everyone remembers the attack on 9/11.

Writing

Choose a topic to write about.

1. Are you a member of any group? It could be a club, a religious group, a sports team, or a group of any type. Write a paragraph of six sentences or more about your experience. Describe the group, and tell when and why you joined it.

2. Write a conversation between a reporter and a Slow Food member or a fast-food lover. Have the reporter ask four or more questions. If you wish, you can begin:

REPORTER: Excuse me. Can I ask you some questions about food?

FAST-FOOD LOVER: Sure.

REPORTER:

Wrap-up

 Match the words with their definitions. There is one extra word.

| accept | bored | boring | disappear | expect | reach |

1. _____ = become impossible to see or find

2. _____ = arrive or get to a place

3. _____ = believe that something will happen

4. _____ = not interesting in any way

5. _____ = decide that someone or something is good
enough

B Complete the sentences with the phrases. There are two extra phrases.

| by magic | figuring out | in general | took part | turn out |
| came out | get to | no doubt | turning it into | |

1. The police say three men _____ in robbing the bank.

2. Barbara is very good at _____ crossword puzzles.

3. Maria has already changed her mind twice and _____
she'll do it again.

4. I hoped to see someone famous on my visit to Hollywood, but I
didn't _____ do that.

5. They are taking a bedroom and _____ a home office.

6. I fell asleep during the movie. How did the story _____?

7. The film *Public Enemy* _____ in 1931.

EXPANDING VOCABULARY

Word Families

Each form of a word belongs to the same **word family**. For example, the noun *danger*, the verb *endanger*, and the adjective *dangerous* all belong to the same word family. Sometimes two members of a word family look the same. That is true for the words *attack*, *mention*, *rush*, and *share*—they can be nouns or verbs.

A The pairs of words in parentheses are members of the same word family. Circle the correct word to complete the sentence. Write *noun* or *verb*.

1. a. You are free to (choice / ⟨choose⟩) the courses you want. ___verb___

    b. He made the (choice / choose) to return to school. _____

2. a. I like (variety / vary) in my food. _____

    b. The dishes on the menu (variety / vary) from day to day. _____

3. a. How much did the baby (weight / weigh)? _____

    b. The nurse checked my (weight / weigh). _____

4. a. What did the scientists (finding / find)? _____

    b. He considered it the most important (finding / find) of his research. _____

5. a. What was the (basis / base) for their disagreement? _____

    b. He's going to (basis / base) his next movie on a comic book. _____

B What part of speech is the **boldfaced** word? Circle *n.* for *noun* or *v.* for *verb*.

1. I didn't hear any **mention** of taxes when the president spoke. *n.* *v.*

2. The dog made a lot of noise, but it didn't **attack**. *n.* *v.*

3. His **share** is the same size as his brother's. *n.* *v.*

4. Don't be in such a **rush**—we have lots of time. *n.* *v.*

A PUZZLE

Complete the sentences with words you studied in Chapters 1–4. Write the words in the puzzle.

Across

1. I know she wants to buy a car, but does she have a ___specific___ car in mind?
4. The _____ of *terrible* is *wonderful*.
5. We need to clean the house. Everything is _____.
8. The cats like to _____ among the plants.
9. The café doesn't _____ dinner, only breakfast and lunch.
11. Naturally, Donna felt _____ after her husband died.

Down

2. You can watch a lot of _____ sports on TV.
3. When the sun comes out, the ice will _____.
6. Peter is _____ 6 feet tall.
7. The _____ person needs 7.5 hours sleep a night.
10. I opened the window to _____ some cool air come in.

BUILDING DICTIONARY SKILLS

Finding Words in the Dictionary, Part 1

Guidewords

Guidewords help you find words in the dictionary. Look at pages 300 and 301 below. The guidewords are *doorman* and *doubtful*. *Doorman* is the first word on the left page; *doubtful* is the last word on the right page.

doorman	300

D

door•man /ˈdɔrmæn, -mən/ *n* plural **doormen** /-mɛn, -mən/ [C] a man who works at the door of a hotel or theater, helping people who are coming in or out

door•mat /ˈdɔrmæt/ *n* [C]
1 a thick piece of material just outside a door for you to clean your shoes on

301	doubtful

D

because you are surprised by what you originally saw or heard

ˈ**double-talk** *n* [U] *disapproving* speech that is complicated, and is intended to deceive or confuse people

ˌ**double ˈvision** *n* [U] a medical condition in which you see two of . . .

A **Will these words be on pages 300–301? Check (✓) *Yes* or *No*.**

	Yes	No
1. dot	☐	☐
2. double	☐	☐
3. doll	☐	☐
4. doubt	☐	☐
5. doughnut	☐	☐
6. dorm	☐	☐

Compound Words

A **compound word** is made up of two words. Some compound words
are written as one word (*birthday, homework*); others are written
as two words (*ice cream, good night*); and others are written with
a hyphen (*good-looking, bird-brained*). The *Longman Dictionary of
American English* treats these words as one word and lists them with
other words in alphabetical order, for example:

good

good evening

good-for-nothing

goodwill

B Write the following words in the order you would find them in the
dictionary.

ice cream	ice-cold	ice
icebreaker	ice cap	ice cream cone

1. _____   4. _____

2. _____   5. _____

3. _____   6. _____

Words with Superscripts

Look at the dictionary entries below. Do you see local[1] and local[2]?
The small, raised numbers are called superscripts. They tell you that
local can be more than one part of speech.

---

lo•cal[1] /ˈloʊkəl/ *adj* **1** [usually before noun] relating to a particular place or area, especially the
place you live in: *a good local hospital* | *The story appeared in the local newspaper.* | *It cost a
quarter to make a **local call*** (=a telephone call to someone in the same area as you). **2** *technical*
affecting a particular part of your body: *a local anesthetic*

local[2] *n* **the locals** the people who live in a particular place

C **What part of speech is *local*?**

It can be an _____ or a _____.

D **Look at these dictionary entries.**

> **tax¹** /tæks/ *n* [C,U] the money you must pay the government, based on how much you earn, what you buy, where you live, etc.: *a 13%* ***tax on*** *cigarettes* | *Everyone who works* ***pays tax***. | *The city will have to* ***raise taxes*** *to pay for the roads.* | *If elected, she promised to* ***cut taxes***. | *I only earn $25,000 a year* ***after taxes*** (=after paying tax). | *a* ***tax increase/cut***
>
> **tax²** *v* [T] **1** to charge a tax on something: *Incomes of under $30,000 are* ***taxed at*** *15%.* **2** **tax sb's patience/strength etc.** to use almost all of someone's PATIENCE, strength, etc.: *His constant questions had begun to tax her patience.*

What part of speech is *tax*? It can be a _____ or a
_____.

Check for superscripts when you look up a word in the dictionary. They tell you that there is more than one entry for a word. It's usually a good idea to read all the meanings and uses of the word.

CHAPTER 5

Teaching and Learning

Fan Hongya in class

GETTING READY TO READ

Talk with a partner or in a small group.

1. What do you see in the photo?

2. Fan Hongya goes by several names. Some people call him Hongya, and some call him Mr. Fan. Others call him Marlin. How many names do you go by? Make a list. Tell who calls you each name.

3. Think of a time of great change in your life. What happened? How did you feel at the time of this change? How do you feel about it now?

READING

Look at the words and definitions next to the reading. Then read without stopping. Don't worry about new words. Don't stop to use a dictionary. Just keep reading!

Teaching and Learning

1   Fan Hongya is standing in front of his class. His students are asking questions about China. "Mr. Fan! Mr. Fan!" they call out.[1] He smiles. "My students are full of questions," he says. "They're curious[2] about different languages and cultures. Here in America, they ask everything! My students back home don't do that—not during class. It was a big change for me."

2   Fan Hongya is from China, where he teaches English in Yangzhou. For a long time, he dreamed about visiting the United States. His dream came true when he received a wonderful **offer**: the chance to teach Chinese in Boston for a year. "It was a great **opportunity** for me," he says. He was very excited about it.

3   He flew to Boston, and a woman from his new school came to **pick him up** at the airport. "Please call me Marlin," he told her. "My American teacher in China gave me this name." They left the airport and drove through Boston while she told him about the city. "She was very **kind** to me," he remembers. "She gave me a wonderful first impression[3] of the people here."

4   A new school year **was about to** begin, so Marlin had little time to get ready. He says, "I wasn't sure what to expect in my classes, but I knew that teaching American kids[4] would be a big **challenge**." The first day of school was exciting for him, but it was also a **shock**.

5   Marlin was used to classes of fifty-five students. In his first class in Boston, there were only three students. One student already spoke Chinese well. The second knew a little Chinese. The third knew nothing **at all**. Marlin thought, "Three different **levels** in one class—how am I going to **deal with** this?!"

6   His second class was big, and the students were quiet and **polite**. They seemed like Chinese students. Time passed quickly, and then **suddenly**, Marlin heard the bell for the end of class. He

[1] *call out* = say in a loud voice

[2] *curious* = interested and wanting to know

[3] a *first impression* = a general feeling about someone or something new

[4] *kids* = (informal) children or teenagers

(continued)

wanted to say a few more words to his students, but they were already out the door! This would never happen in China.

7   The next few weeks were difficult for Marlin. He missed his wife and daughter, and he did not know how to deal with his classes. It made him feel terrible. Students in Boston seemed completely different from students in China, and Marlin was almost ready to **quit**. He was very **disappointed** with his "dream come true."

8   It took some time, but after a while, Marlin adjusted to[5] the school and his students. He began to enjoy his classes, and his students learned to love him. At the end of the year, he would return to China with happy **memories** of his experience in Boston and his students there—with all their questions.

[5] *adjusted to* = made small changes and got used to something

Quick Comprehension Check

Read these sentences. Circle T (true) or F (false).

1. Fan Hongya and Marlin Fan are two names for the same person.   T   F

2. Marlin teaches Chinese in China.   T   F

3. He got the chance to teach in the United States for one year.   T   F

4. His school in Boston was just as he expected.   T   F

5. His wife and daughter were in Boston with him.   T   F

6. Marlin says Chinese and American students are the same in every way.   T   F

EXPLORING VOCABULARY

Thinking about the Target Vocabulary

 A Find the six nouns in **bold** in "Teaching and Learning." Add them to the chart. Write them in the order they appear in the reading. Use the singular form of any plural noun.

	Nouns	Verbs	Adjectives	Other
2				
3		pick someone up		
			kind	
4		be about to		
5				at all
		deal with		
6			polite	
				suddenly
7		quit		
			disappointed	
8				

B Which words are new to you? Circle them in the chart. Then find the words in the reading. Look at the context. Can you guess the meaning?

Using the Target Vocabulary

 These sentences are about the reading. Complete them with the target words and phrases in the box.

at all	deal with	memories	polite	suddenly
challenge	level	picked him up	shock	was about to

1. It was almost time for the new school year to begin. The school year _____ start.

2. A woman from the school went to the airport in her car. She met Marlin and gave him a ride. She _____.

3. Teaching in Boston would be exciting but difficult for him. It would be a big _____.

4. The first day of school was very, very surprising to Marlin. It was a _____.

5. One student knew no Chinese. The student didn't know any Chinese _____. (Add this phrase to make a negative stronger.)

6. Marlin was in the middle of teaching. He wasn't thinking about the end of class. Then _____, class was over.

7. In one class, all the students were beginners. They were all at the same _____.

8. Marlin didn't know what to do with his classes at first. He didn't know how to _____ them.

9. The students in Marlin's second class listened quietly and acted like nice people. They seemed _____.

10. Marlin will remember Boston with a smile. He will have happy _____ of his experience.

B These sentences use the target words and phrases **in new contexts.**
Complete them with the words and phrases in the box.

| at all | deal with | memories | polite | suddenly |
| challenge | level | pick you up | shock | were about to |

1. It's a parent's job to teach his or her children to be _____.
2. Our dinner turned out to be much more expensive than we expected.
   The cost came as a _____.
3. I like to look at old photos of my friends. The pictures bring back
   good _____.
4. We went to find our friends and say good-bye. They
   _____ leave for the airport.
5. When you take a course, do you want it to be really easy? Or do you
   like a _____?
6. I can't play tennis with him. He's too good. I'm not at his
   _____.
7. We were in the car, driving along, and then _____, a cat
   ran into the street.
8. Bob and Sonia had trouble planning their wedding. They had to
   _____ many problems.
9. What time does your train arrive? I can come and _____.
10. I don't know her _____. We've never even met.

Read these sentences. Match the boldfaced target words with their definitions.

a. Jane hates her job, so she's going to **quit**.

b. He has a new job **opportunity**. Will he take it? He has to decide soon.

c. When is "Be **Kind** to Animals Week"?

d. He was **disappointed** when nobody laughed at his joke.

e. They said, "Would you like a ride?" and I was happy to accept their **offer**.

Target Words	Definitions
1. _____	= nice, helpful, friendly, and caring
2. _____	= leave a job, school, etc., especially because it makes you unhappy
3. _____	= a chance to do something or a time when it is possible
4. _____	= a statement from someone who wants to help
5. _____	= sad because something didn't happen (or didn't turn out well)

Building on the Vocabulary: Word Grammar

Count nouns have singular and plural forms: a *pen*, *two pens*; *a man*, *two men*.

Noncount nouns (or *uncountable nouns*) have only one form: *air*, *water*, *music*. Do not use *a*, *an*, or a number with a noncount noun.

Some nouns can be both count and noncount nouns. The meanings may be different, as in these examples:

Count Nouns	Noncount Nouns
I called you three **times** and left messages.	How much **time** do we have before class?
Winning that game was an **experience** I'll never forget.	He won't get the job because he has no **experience**.

A Look at the **boldfaced** nouns. Circle C (count) or U (uncountable) for each one.

1. She has good **memories** from her old school.   C   U

2. He has a good **memory** for names. (He doesn't
   forget them.)   C   U

3. How much **memory** does your computer have?   C   U

B Complete these sentences. Use *memory* or *memories*.

1. I have a terrible _____ for numbers.

2. This computer has three gigabytes of _____.

3. She has bad _____ of learning to swim.

C On a piece of paper, write two sentences with *memory* and *memories*.

DEVELOPING YOUR SKILLS

Reading for Details

Are these statements about the reading true or false? If the reading doesn't give the information, check (✓) *It doesn't say.*

	True	False	It doesn't say.
1. Marlin looked forward to traveling to Boston.	☐	☐	☐
2. He had the chance to take his family with him but decided not to.	☐	☐	☐
3. He had friends from the United States in China.	☐	☐	☐
4. He expected teaching in Boston to be easy.	☐	☐	☐
5. Marlin's students in Boston were interested in China.	☐	☐	☐
6. Marlin's Chinese students are usually quiet and polite.	☐	☐	☐
7. Marlin quit his teaching job in Boston.	☐	☐	☐
8. Marlin had a good school year.	☐	☐	☐

Main Ideas

What is the main idea of paragraph 7 in the reading? Check (✓) your answer.

☐ **1.** Marlin was unhappy during the first part of the school year in Boston.

☐ **2.** Marlin was a terrible teacher and could not deal with his classes in Boston.

☐ **3.** Marlin missed his wife and daughter because they were back home in China.

Summarizing

Write a summary of "Teaching and Learning." Write it as a paragraph. Include answers to these questions:

• Who is Marlin Fan (or Fan Hongya)? Where is he from? What does he do?

• What did Marlin used to dream about? What did he get the chance to do?

• What was it like for him at first? Why?

• How did it turn out in the end?

If you wish, you can begin your paragraph Fan Hongya is an English teacher from Yangzhou, China. He used to . . .

Role-Play

Work with a partner. Imagine that one of you is Marlin and one of you is his wife. You are talking on the phone. It is the first week of the school year in Boston. What will Marlin say about his experiences at school? What questions will he and his wife have for each other?

Using New Words

Work with a partner. Choose five target words or phrases from the chart on page 53. On a piece of paper, use each word or phrase in a sentence.

Writing

Choose a topic. Write a paragraph of eight sentences or more.

1. What part of learning English is a challenge for you? Complete the sentence below. Then give your reasons.

    Sometimes learning English is hard. It is a challenge for me to . . .

2. Do you have happy memories of a trip? Write about it. If you wish, you can begin: *I have happy memories of a trip to . . .*

CHAPTER 6

"It Was Love, So Strong and So Real"

Arunaa

GETTING READY TO READ

Talk with a partner.

1. You're going to read a love story. It's about two people from opposite sides of the world. What are some possible challenges for them?

2. How important is it for married people to have things in common[1] with each other? Choose a number between 1 (extremely important) and 4 (not important at all). Explain your answer.

[1] *have things in common* = share the same interests, experiences, beliefs, etc.

READING

Look at the words and definitions next to the reading. Then read without stopping.

"It Was Love, So Strong and So Real"

1   Arunaa was in her last year of college near her home in Malaysia. It was the first day of a new course, and she was in class. "Suddenly," she says, "I had this **awful** feeling of being watched." She looked across the room. Someone was **staring** at her—an exchange student[1] from Europe. He **went on** looking at her all through the class. He did it the next day, too, and the next. Finally, she told herself, "Enough! I'm going to talk to him. That will stop him." So she went and sat down next to him. She **discovered** that his name was Hervé, and he was French. "As soon as we started talking, it was magic and he was perfect."

[1] an *exchange student* = someone who studies for a while at a foreign university

2   Arunaa and Hervé fell in love. But after a few months, he had to return to France. Soon afterwards, Arunaa graduated and **faced** the biggest decision of her life. Hervé wanted her to join him in Paris. Should she go, or should she try to forget him?

3   Arunaa remembers, "My parents were in **total** shock. But the best thing was that they never said no. It was always my choice and my **responsibility**. This is what they always taught me, to make my own decisions."

4   It was hard for Arunaa to think of leaving family, friends, and home. Living in France would be a challenge, too. For one thing, she did not speak French. "And it was difficult for me," she says, "because I wasn't really sure what to expect. When I met Hervé, he was a student, and almost like a tourist.[2] He was happy in Malaysia and he felt **comfortable** there, but that wasn't real life for him. I was about to meet another Hervé, whom I didn't know—the Hervé who was **no longer** a student, but a man with a serious job, and a Frenchman in his own country."

[2] a *tourist* = someone who is traveling for fun

5   Arunaa decided to go. "I had to take the chance.[3] **Although** there were many **differences** between us, we were so much

[3] *take the chance* = do something that may be dangerous

(continued)

alike! I knew that he was the one for me." For Arunaa and Hervé, it was the right decision. Now they are happily married.

6   **Marriage** is not easy. It is even harder when a **couple** has to deal with differences in language, religion, and culture. Arunaa says, "The cultural differences were enormous.[4] I come from an Islamic country, although my family is Christian, and many things in France shocked me." The hardest thing, she says, is to understand the way that French people think.

[4] *enormous* = very, very big

7   Smaller differences in their everyday life caused problems, too. Arunaa laughs, "We are like night and day![5] I eat rice three times a day, and I don't wear shoes in the house. Also, I want to take care of my husband, like my mother and her mother before her, but that makes Hervé uncomfortable." Even with all the **difficulties**, after seven years, they are still very much in love.

[5] *like night and day* = complete opposites

Quick Comprehension Check

Read these sentences. Circle T (true) or F (false).

1. Arunaa is a young woman from Malaysia.   T   F

2. She met Hervé when she was a college student in France.   T   F

3. Arunaa's parents told her not to leave home.   T   F

4. Arunaa and Hervé are now married and living in France.   T   F

5. It was hard for Arunaa to get used to many things in her new life.   T   F

EXPLORING VOCABULARY

Thinking about the Target Vocabulary

 A Find the four verbs in **bold** in "'It Was Love, So Strong and So Real.'" Add them to the chart. Use the base form of each verb.

	Nouns	Verbs	Adjectives	Other
1			awful	
2				
3			total	
	responsibility			
4			comfortable	
				no longer
5				although
	difference			
			alike	
6	marriage			
	couple			
7	difficulty			

B Which words are new to you? Circle them in the chart. Then find the words in the reading. Look at the context. Can you guess the meaning?

Using the Target Vocabulary

 A These sentences are **about the reading**. What is the meaning of each **boldfaced** word or phrase? Circle a, b, or c.

1. Arunaa saw someone new across the room. He was **staring** at her. *Stare* means

   a. speak, talk.   **b.** point a finger.   **c.** keep looking.

2. The exchange student **went on** looking at Arunaa, day after day. *Go on* means

   a. stop.   **b.** continue.   **c.** disappear.

3. She talked to him and **discovered** that he was French. *Discover* means
   a. find out, learn.   **b.** tell, say.   **c.** consider.

4. Arunaa had to **face** a big decision. *Face* means
   a. turn into.   **b.** deal with.   **c.** turn out.

5. Hervé felt **comfortable** in Malaysia. It was good to be there. If you are comfortable, you are
   a. stressed.   **b.** bored.   **c.** feeling good.

6. **Although** there were many differences between Arunaa and Hervé, they were the same in important ways. Use *although* to introduce the first part of a sentence when the second part
   a. gives a reason.   **b.** repeats the first part.   **c.** may seem surprising.

7. Arunaa says they are different in some ways but **alike** in others. *Alike* means
   a. the same or nearly the same.   **b.** disappointed, unhappy.   **c.** the opposite.

8. Arunaa and Hervé are married. They have a good **marriage**. *Marriage* means
   a. a plan for the future.   **b.** the relationship between a husband and wife.   **c.** a memory of the past.

9. This is the story of a **couple** from two different cultures. *A couple* means
   a. a change in ideas and traditions.   **b.** two people in a relationship.   **c.** a problem or trouble.

10. It's not easy to be married. There are even more **difficulties** in cross-cultural marriages. *Difficulty* means something that is
    a. fun.   **b.** hard.   **c.** new.

B These sentences use the target words and phrases **in new contexts**. Complete them with the words and phrases in the box.

alike	comfortable	difficulties	face	marriage
although	couple	discovered	go on	stare

1. We looked out the window and _____ that it was snowing.

2. In my country, it's not polite to _____ at people. What about in yours?

3. _____ he's not tall, he's a good basketball player.

4. Finally, the judge said to the _____, "You are now husband and wife."

5. Good communication between husband and wife is important for a strong _____.

6. You can't run away from this problem. You have to _____ it.

7. Suddenly, the TV screen went black and a voice said, "We are experiencing technical _____."

8. I was _____ in bed, and I didn't want to get up.

9. She and her sister look _____, but they dress very differently.

10. We can't afford to _____ spending money like this. We have to stop.

Read each definition and look at the paragraph number. Look back at the reading on pages 61–62 to find the **boldfaced** word or phrase to match the definition. Copy it in the chart.

Definition	Paragraph	Target Word or Phrase
1. very bad, terrible	1	
2. complete	3	
3. something you have to do or take care of	3	
4. not now, not anymore	4	
5. ways that two people or things are not like each other	5	

Building on the Vocabulary: Word Grammar

Go on is a **phrasal verb**. Phrasal verbs have two parts: a verb (such as *make*, *get*, or *turn*) and a particle (such as *up*, *out*, or *off*).

The meaning of the phrasal verb is different from the meanings of its two parts. For example, *dealing with* something (such as a problem or a difficult person) is different from *dealing* something (such as cards in a card game).

A Complete each sentence with a phrasal verb. Use *come out, deal with, figure out, go on, pick up, turn into,* or *turn out*. There is one extra verb.

1. Work, classes, taking care of your children—that's a lot for you to

   _____!

2. Luis is driving to the airport to _____ his parents.

3. I'm sure everything will _____ well in the end.

4. Their discussions sometimes _____ fights.

5. We need help. We can't _____ what to do.

6. I'm sure he won't quit. He'll _____ trying.

B On a piece of paper, write three sentences with phrasal verbs from Part A.

DEVELOPING YOUR SKILLS

Identifying Paragraph Topics

What is each paragraph in the reading about? Write the topics of the paragraphs.

1. Paragraph 1: _how Arunaa and Harvé met_

2. Paragraph 2: _____

3. Paragraph 3: _____

4. Paragraph 4: _____

5. Paragraph 5: _____

6. Paragraph 6: _____

7. Paragraph 7: _____

Reading for Details

Are these statements about the reading true or false? If the reading doesn't give the information, check (✓) "It doesn't say."

	True	False	It doesn't say.
1. Arunaa met Hervé in a college classroom in Malaysia.	☐	☐	☐
2. Hervé left before Arunaa graduated.	☐	☐	☐
3. Arunaa expected him to come back.	☐	☐	☐
4. Arunaa's parents told her not to go to France.	☐	☐	☐
5. Hervé expected things to be easy for her in France.	☐	☐	☐
6. Arunaa says her biggest challenge was religious differences.	☐	☐	☐
7. In France, Arunaa still eats rice three times a day.	☐	☐	☐
8. Arunaa can speak French well now.	☐	☐	☐

Reading Between the Lines

"Reading between the lines" means understanding meaning that is hidden or is not given openly. Readers have to make **inferences**—guesses that they base on the information given and what they already know.

Answer these questions with your own opinions.

1. Why was Hervé staring at Arunaa in class? _____

   _____

2. Why were Arunaa's parents in shock? _____

   _____

3. What worried Arunaa most when she thought about going to France?

   _____

4. Why doesn't Arunaa wear shoes in the house? _____

   _____

5. Why is Hervé uncomfortable with the way that Arunaa wants to take care of him? _____

   _____

Sharing Opinions

Talk about the following opinions in a small group. Tell why you agree or disagree.

Opinion 1: Your parents' opinion of the person you marry is very important.

Opinion 2: People should decide for themselves about marriage. They—and not their families—should have total responsibility for the decision.

Opinion 3: It's better to marry someone who is as much like you as possible.

Using New Words

Work with a partner. Choose five target words or phrases from the chart on page 63. On a piece of paper, use each word or phrase in a sentence.

Writing

Choose a topic.

1. What questions would you like to ask Arunaa or Hervé? Write a list of five or more questions.

2. Do you believe in love at first sight (falling in love the first time you see someone)? Write a paragraph of eight sentences or more. If you wish, you can begin: I (believe/don't believe) in love at first sight because . . .

3. When did you face a big decision in your life? What did you decide? How do you feel about it now? Write a paragraph of eight sentences or more.

CHAPTER 7

To Live as an Artist

Vitek Kruta talking about painting

GETTING READY TO READ

Vitek Kruta was born in communist[1] Czechoslovakia.* Work in small groups. Look at the countries in this list. Which ones have, or used to have, a communist government? Check (✓) your answers.

	In the Past	Now	Never
a. Russia			
b. China			
c. Japan			
d. Spain			
e. Cuba			

[1] *communist* = having total government control of all land, factories, food production, schools, etc.

* *In 1993, Czechoslovakia became two independent countries: the Czech Republic and Slovakia.*

READING

Look at the pictures, words, and definitions next to the reading. Then read without stopping.

To Live as an Artist

1   In 1981, the artist Vitek Kruta **escaped** from his country. He left with just one little bag. "One little bag with basic things like a toothbrush and underwear," he remembers. He was nineteen years old at the time.

2   Vitek's home was in Prague, Czechoslovakia. He loved his country, but he could not stay there because the communist government wanted to put him in jail.[1] "The government wanted total **control** of all art and music," he **explains**. "We had to have art shows in secret. My kind of painting was **against** the law. The rock music that my band played was against the law. There was no future for me there." So Vitek escaped to Germany. The rest of his family was still in Prague, and after he left, the police made a lot of trouble for his father.

3   In Germany, Vitek first had to learn the language. He spoke Czech and Russian but not German, so he spent eight months taking **lessons** at a language school. Vitek remembers that it was easy for him to understand and read German, but he could not speak it. Then one night, he had a dream. In his dream, he was skiing[2] in the mountains. He met another skier and started talking with him—in German! The following day, he discovered that he could speak much better.

4   Next, Vitek **got back to** his studies in art. He learned to restore[3] old buildings such as churches and castles.[4] He spent ten years doing this kind of work, and then he faced another big change in his life: He got a job offer in the United States. Vitek knew **hardly** any English, but he did not let that stop him. **After all**, he had **a great deal** of experience learning new languages. So he and his wife, Lucie, decided to make the move.

5   Today, Vitek is a painter, an architect,[5] and much more. He is a man with a lot of **energy**. He works in his studio,[6] he teaches art classes, and he helps **manage** an art school.

(continued)

[1] *jail* = a room or building where the police can hold someone

[2] *skiing*

[3] *restore* = make new again

[4] a *castle*

[5] an *architect* = a person whose job is planning and designing buildings

[6] a *studio* = the workplace of an artist

6   Vitek also likes to bring together people with different **talents** and abilities to do big art **projects**. Sometimes he has a group work on restoring a building. Sometimes they **cover** a room with murals (large pictures painted on the walls). Vitek likes to do these projects in public places—at schools or in city buildings or in churches—so that anyone can see and enjoy them. He says that projects like these "bring art back to the people."

7   Vitek believes that art must have an important place in our lives. Art lets people be creative,[7] and the world needs creative people. Vitek explains, "If we are not free to be creative—and I'm talking about scientists and mathematicians, too, not just artists—then human beings can only copy the past. We cannot move **forward**."

[7] *creative* = good at thinking of and making new things

Quick Comprehension Check

Read these sentences. Circle T (true) or F (false).

1. Vitek grew up in communist Czechoslovakia.   T   F

2. At age nineteen, he was in danger of going to jail.   T   F

3. Now he lives and works in the United States.   T   F

4. He is uncomfortable sharing his art with other people.   T   F

5. Vitek thinks that no one really needs art, but it's fun.   T   F

EXPLORING VOCABULARY

Thinking about the Target Vocabulary

 A Find the five nouns and five verbs in **bold** in "To Live as an Artist." Add them to the chart. Use the singular form of any plural noun and the base form of each verb.

	Nouns	Verbs	Adjectives	Other
1				
2				
				against
3				
4				
				hardly
				after all
				a great deal
5				
6				
7				forward

 B Which words are new to you? Circle them in the chart. Then find the words in the reading. Look at the context. Can you guess the meaning?

Using the Target Vocabulary

 These sentences are **about the reading**. Complete them with the target words and phrases in the box.

after all	control	escaped	got back to	manage
a great deal	covers	forward	hardly	projects

1. In 1981, people were not free to leave Czechoslovakia when they wanted to, so Vitek had to leave secretly. He _____.

2. Artists and musicians in Czechoslovakia were not free to do what they wanted. The government wanted _____ of all art and music.

3. Vitek had to stop studying art for a while and study German. Then he _____ studying art.

4. Vitek knew _____ any English before moving to the United States. He knew almost none.

5. Vitek knew little English, but he still decided to move to the United States. _____, he'd had a lot of practice learning new languages. (Use this phrase to introduce a fact that someone should remember or consider.)

6. Vitek had _____ of experience as a language learner. He had already learned Russian and German (and of course Czech, his first language).

7. Today Vitek helps _____ an art school. He is one of the decision makers for the school.

8. Vitek sometimes paints murals. A mural is a large painting that is painted on a wall. It _____ a whole wall.

9. Vitek likes to do art _____ in places that anyone can enter. These are carefully planned pieces of work that often take a long time.

10. He believes human beings shouldn't stay as we are now. We should move _____ with new ideas.

B These sentences use the target words and phrases **in new contexts**. Complete them with the words and phrases in the box.

after all	control	escape	get back to	manages
a great deal	covered	forward	hardly	projects

1. Olivia owns and _____ the company. Ten people work for her.

2. The plan for building the new school cannot go _____ without more money.

3. Snow fell during the night. It completely _____ the ground.

4. On an icy road, a driver can lose _____ of his or her car.

5. The fifth grade students spent weeks working on their science _____.

6. Steven's boss told him to get off the phone and _____ work.

7. The message was very short. It _____ said anything at all.

8. Randy knows a lot about taxes. He knows _____ more than I do.

9. The cat has to stay inside, so please close the door or she might _____.

10. Ann doesn't seem at all worried about having the baby, but _____, this will be her third.

C Read these sentences. Match the **boldfaced** target words with their definitions on page 76.

a. His parents discovered his musical **talent** when he was very young.

b. The children were full of **energy**, and they played for hours in the park.

c. I don't understand the homework. I'll ask the teacher to **explain** it.

d. Children can't drive. It's **against** the law.

e. She wants to learn to fly a plane, so she's taking flying **lessons**.

Target Words	Definitions
1. _____	= times that someone works with a teacher to learn a skill
2. _____	= a natural ability to do something well
3. _____	= the power of body and mind that lets you be active and do things
4. _____	= talk about something so it's clear and easy to understand
5. _____	= in disagreement with or opposed to (rules, laws, etc.)

Building on the Vocabulary: Word Grammar

Hardly and *hard* are very different.

*He works **hard**.* = He puts a lot of energy into his work.

*He **hardly** ever works.* = He almost never works.

Hardly usually comes before the main verb. It has a negative meaning ("almost not"). Do not use it with another negative word:

I hardly never see her.

A **Rewrite these sentences using *hardly*.**

1. We almost couldn't see the plane. <u>We could hardly see the plane.</u>
2. I almost can't hear you. _____
3. He almost never cries. _____
4. They almost never speak in class. _____

B **Write two sentences with *hard* and *hardly*.**

1. _____
2. _____

DEVELOPING YOUR SKILLS

Scanning

Read these questions about "To Live as an Artist." Scan the reading and write answers in complete sentences.

1. Who is Vitek Kruta? _____

2. Where did he grow up? _____

3. When did he escape? _____

4. What did he take with him? _____

   _____

5. How old was he at the time? _____

6. Where did he go first? _____

7. Where does he live now? _____

8. What languages does he know now? _____

   _____

9. What are three examples of the type of work Vitek does? _____

   _____

10. Why does Vitek think art should have an important place in our

    lives? _____

    _____

Main Ideas

What is the main idea of paragraph 2 in the reading? Check (✓) your answer.

☐ **1.** Vitek grew up in the city of Prague in communist Czechoslovakia, but he left for Germany.

☐ **2.** Vitek left Czechoslovakia because the government would not let him be free to live as an artist.

☐ **3.** Back in 1981, the Czechoslovakian government wanted total control of all artists and musicians.

Reading Between the Lines

To answer these questions, tell what you think is true, based on information in the reading. Give the reasons for your answers.

1. Did Vitek ask the government to let him leave Czechoslovakia?

   _____

   _____

2. Is Vitek good at dealing with changes in his life? _____

   _____

   _____

3. Is Vitek living the life he dreamed of when he was a young man?

   _____

   _____

Discussion

Talk about these questions in a small group.

1. What were the big changes in Vitek's life that are described in the reading?

2. Some people leave their countries because they don't have any other choice. Do you know anyone who had to leave his or her country? Tell what happened.

3. Think about going to live in another country without knowing the language. What is the hardest part of a move like that?

4. Does art have a place in your life? Explain.

Using New Words

Work with a partner. Choose five target words or phrases from the chart on page 73. On a piece of paper, use each word or phrase in a sentence.

Writing

Do you know someone who had to leave his or her country, someone who has a special talent, or someone who is full of energy? Write a paragraph of eight sentences or more about this person. If you wish, you can begin: I want to tell you about . . .

CHAPTER 8

An Amazing Woman

Ruth Simmons, president of Brown University

GETTING READY TO READ

Talk in a small group or with your whole class.

1. What can you guess about the woman in the photo?

2. You will read about big changes in Ruth Simmons's life. You will also read about changes in the United States during the last fifty years. Think about your country fifty years ago. What is one thing that is now very different?

Complete this sentence:

Fifty years ago in my country, _____,

but now _____.

READING

Look at the words and definitions next to the reading. Then read without stopping.

An Amazing Woman

1   Ruth Simmons was born in a very poor family. Today, she is the president of a famous university. How did she do it? Hers is an **amazing** story.

2   The story begins on a farm in Grapeland, Texas, in 1945, the year that Ruth was born. Her parents were farmworkers, and she was the youngest of their twelve children. They could not give their children many things, and Ruth never had any **toys**. For Christmas, she did not receive any presents at all **except** a shoe box with an apple, an orange, and some nuts. However, in Grapeland, Ruth was not really **aware** of being poor because no one else had much, either. Then the family moved into the city, to Houston, where being poor was much harder. In school, other children laughed at the way she spoke and dressed.

3   Ruth's mother kept the family together. She had no education, "but she was very **wise**," Ruth remembers. "She taught us about the real **value** of being a human being, what **mattered** and what didn't matter." Ruth's mother did not have big dreams. She just wanted to see her children grow up. This was not a simple wish. At that time, there was segregation[1] in the United States, and life was dangerous for African Americans, especially in the South.[2] Ruth remembers living in **fear**. "If you looked at someone the wrong way, you could be killed."

4   At age five, Ruth fell in love with school. She was a **bright** child, and she was lucky to have some excellent teachers. No one in Ruth's family had much education, but her teachers **encouraged** her to go to college, and Ruth was **brave** enough to try. They also gave her money and even a coat to wear.

5   At first, Ruth studied theater,[3] but what kind of **career** could a young African American woman hope for? She says, "Remember I grew up in the South; I couldn't even go to theaters."[3] So she studied languages instead. Later, she married,

[1] *segregation* = laws that kept black people from using the same schools, hotels, restaurants, etc., as white people

[2] *the South* = the southern states where whites had black slaves from the 1600s until 1863

[3] *theater* = (a) reading, writing, and acting in plays; (b) a place where you see a movie or a play

had two children, began a teaching career, and became a college administrator.[4] Soon people began to **notice** her and respect her abilities.

[4] an *administrator* = a manager in the government, a school, a business, etc.

6   In 1995, Ruth became president of Smith College, a famous U.S. college for women. Ruth was the first African American to **lead** a college like this one. Suddenly, her story was on TV and in newspapers all over the country. Six years later, she accepted another challenge. She became the president of Brown University.

7   Ruth believes in the **power** of education. "Learning can be the same for a poor farm kid like me as it is for the richest child in the country. It's all about cultivating one's mind,[5] and anybody can do that. So it doesn't matter what color your skin is, it doesn't matter how much money your father has, it doesn't matter what kind of house you live in. Every learner can experience the same thing." As President Simmons will tell you, education can change your life.

[5] *cultivating one's mind* = helping your mind to grow

President Simmons's words come from "Poised for the Presidency" by Judith Gingerich and Sarah Curran Barrett, Smith Alumnae Quarterly, *Winter 1995/96. The final quotation has been simplified.*

Quick Comprehension Check

Read these sentences. Circle T (true) or F (false).

1. Ruth Simmons is the president of a famous university.   T   F

2. She grew up in a very poor family.   T   F

3. While she was growing up, she always planned to go to college.   T   F

4. She grew up during a dangerous time for black Americans.   T   F

5. She always wanted a career as a college president.   T   F

6. Ruth's message is, "Education can change any person's life."   T   F

EXPLORING VOCABULARY

Thinking about the Target Vocabulary

 A   Find the four verbs and five adjectives in **bold** in "An Amazing Woman." Add them to the chart. Use the base form of each verb.

	Nouns	Verbs	Adjectives	Other
1				
2	toy			
				except
3				
	value			
	fear			
4				
5	career			
6				
7	power			

B   Which words are new to you? Circle them in the chart. Then find the words in the reading. Look at the context. Can you guess the meaning?

Using the Target Vocabulary

 A   These sentences are **about the reading**. What is the meaning of each **boldfaced** word? Circle a, b, or c.

1. Ruth Simmons has had a very unusual life. Her life story is **amazing**. *Amazing* means

   a. common and expected.

   b. surprising and wonderful.

   c. slow and boring.

2. At first, being poor wasn't important to her. Ruth wasn't **aware** of being poor. *Aware of something* means
   a. happy about it and proud of it.
   b. excited about it.
   c. knowing and thinking about it.

3. Although she had no education, Ruth's mother was very **wise**. *Wise* means
   a. able to make good decisions.
   b. afraid of many things.
   c. polite to other people.

4. Ruth's mother taught her children the true **value** of things in life. The value of a thing is
   a. where it comes from.
   b. its history.
   c. how much it's worth.

5. Ruth learned from her mother what to care about—what does and does not **matter** in life. Things that matter are
   a. average.
   b. natural.
   c. important.

6. Ruth and many other African Americans lived in **fear** of being killed. Fear is
   a. the feeling of being afraid.
   b. a memory of something.
   c. a place or an area.

7. Ruth was a **bright** child, so she did well in school. *Bright* means
   a. hungry.
   b. intelligent.
   c. angry.

8. She was nervous about college. She had to be **brave** to try it. *Brave* means
   a. ready to face danger.
   b. too afraid to do something.
   c. crazy, like a fool.

9. People noticed Ruth's abilities and respected her work. *Notice* means
   a. produce or make.
   b. become aware of.
   c. joke about.

10. Ruth now **leads** a famous U.S. university. She is the president. *Lead* means
    a. study or learn.
    b. discover or find out.
    c. show others what to do.

B These sentences use the target words **in new contexts**. Complete them with the words in the box.

amazing	brave	fear	matter	value
aware	bright	lead	noticed	wise

1. You don't have to rush. It doesn't _____ if we get there late.
2. He's a fast learner. He's very _____.
3. People expect firefighters to be _____.
4. I wasn't _____ of the problem. Please explain it to me.
5. The cat _____ the bird and stared at it.
6. We all understand the _____ of a good education.
7. People often go to him for advice. He's a very _____ man.
8. You can speak six languages? That's _____!
9. You know the way to go, so you _____ and we'll follow.
10. Many people are afraid to fly. Many others have a _____ of public speaking.

C Read these sentences. Match the **boldfaced** target words with their definitions.

a. I **encourage** her to call us if she has any problem.
b. The president has the **power** and the responsibility to lead the country.
c. Peter had a long **career** as a researcher.
d. The little boy received some **toys** and games as birthday presents.
e. Everyone is here today **except** Jamal. He's sick.

Target Words   **Definitions**

1. _____ = things for children to play with

2. _____ = not including, besides

3. _____ = the ability to control people and events and make changes

4. _____ = the years of someone's life spent working in a profession

5. _____ = say or do things to help a person feel confident enough to try something

Building on the Vocabulary: Word Grammar

Value has several meanings. It can be a count noun, a noncount noun, or a verb. Read these definitions:

value n. [U] the importance or usefulness of something

values n. pl. a person's ideas about what is right and wrong and what is important in life

value v. think that (something) is important

Complete these sentences with *value* or *values*.

1. I _____ her as a friend.
2. He understands the _____ of this opportunity.
3. We have a lot in common, and we share the same _____.

DEVELOPING YOUR SKILLS

Reading for Details

Are these statements about the reading true or false? If the reading doesn't give the information, check (✓) *It doesn't say*.

		True	False	It doesn't say.
1.	Ruth Simmons was born in the United States.	☐	☐	☐
2.	She had younger brothers and sisters.	☐	☐	☐
3.	As a child, she was aware of the dangers for black Americans.	☐	☐	☐
4.	She enjoyed school and was successful there.	☐	☐	☐
5.	Ruth's parents encouraged her to go to college.	☐	☐	☐
6.	Her teachers helped her go to college.	☐	☐	☐
7.	She felt that planning a career in theater was a wise idea for her.	☐	☐	☐
8.	She studied at Harvard University.	☐	☐	☐
9.	She became the first woman to lead a famous U.S. college.	☐	☐	☐
10.	Her story was on TV.	☐	☐	☐

Summarizing

Write a summary of "An Amazing Woman." Write it as a paragraph. Include the answers to these questions:

- Who is Ruth Simmons?
- What was her childhood like?
- What is unusual about her life story?
- What does she believe in?

If you wish, you can begin:

> Ruth Simmons is an African American woman and the president of Brown University in the United States. She grew up . . .

Discussion

Talk about these questions in a small group.

1. The title of the reading in this chapter is "An Amazing Woman." What does that mean? Is it a good title for Ruth Simmons's life story? Why?

2. Ruth's teachers encouraged her to go to college. Who encourages you? What do they encourage you to do? Why?

3. Ruth has strong ideas about what's right and what's wrong, and what matters and what doesn't matter. These beliefs are her values. She learned her values from her mother. Where did you learn your values? How did you learn them?

Using New Words

Work with a partner. Choose five target words from the chart on page 82. On a piece of paper, use each target word in a sentence.

Writing

Choose Discussion question 2 or 3 from above. Write a paragraph. If you wish, you can begin:

_____ encourage(s) me to _____. (He/She/They) always tell(s) me . . .
or
I learned my values from _____. (He/She/They) taught me to . . .

Wrap-up

REVIEWING VOCABULARY

 A Think about the types of words in each group. Are they nouns, verbs, or adjectives? Cross out the word that does not belong.

1. couple   ~~wise~~   memory   responsibility

2. toy   discover   pick up   explain

3. polite   bright   awful   career

4. energy   difficulty   suddenly   marriage

5. quit   stare   difference   manage

6. aware   brave   offer   alike

 B Complete the sentences with words or phrases from the box. There are two extra words or phrases.

after all	a great deal	at all	fear	hardly
against	although	except	forward	no longer

1. It is _____ the law not to pay your taxes.

2. _____ he was tired, he went on studying.

3. Aren't you hungry? You ate _____ anything.

4. Everyone in the class is here _____ Kimiko.

5. We should get her a present. _____, she's been very kind to us.

6. It used to be important to me, but it _____ matters.

7. We can't go back. We can only go _____.

8. That painter has _____ of talent.

EXPANDING VOCABULARY

Complete the chart with the **boldfaced** members of each word family. Use the singular form of any plural noun and the base form of each verb.

	Nouns	Verbs	Adjectives
1.	amazement	amaze	
2.			
3.			
4.			
5.			
6.			
7.			
8.			

1. **a.** The magic show **amazed** everyone.

   b. I stared out the window in **amazement**.

   c. We've seen an **amazing** change in her.

2. **a.** He **challenged** his brother to a race.

   b. My new job will be a big **challenge**.

   c. It's a **challenging** game, and I need more practice.

3. **a.** These are **comfortable** shoes.

   b. The mother **comforted** the child.

   c. The hotel tries to offer all the **comforts** of home.

4. **a.** He promised we would not be **disappointed**.

   b. They'll just have to deal with the **disappointment**.

   c. I'm afraid I'll **disappoint** them.

5. **a.** The doctor gave us some **encouraging** news.

   b. My friends **encouraged** me to get up and dance.

   c. All he needs is a little **encouragement**.

6. **a.** Please **lead** the way.

   b. She's an experienced **leader**.

   c. What's the **leading** cause of car accidents?

7. **a.** What a **shocking** story!

   b. The news came as a **shock**.

   c. She **shocked** her parents with her green hair.

8. **a.** He lost a **valuable** ring.

   b. I **value** your opinion very much.

   c. His research is of great **value** to heart patients everywhere.

A PUZZLE

There are 10 target words from Unit 2 in this puzzle. The words go across (→) and down (↓). Find the words and circle them. Then use them to complete the sentences below.

X	Z	P	M	X	M	L	E	V	E	L
K	N	O	T	I	C	E	V	X	K	E
L	X	W	B	Q	M	X	J	Z	H	S
J	N	E	P	X	N	Q	M	V	P	S
Q	U	R	P	M	A	T	T	E	R	O
L	E	A	D	G	X	H	X	K	O	N
X	S	Z	T	V	M	W	G	T	J	N
M	C	O	V	E	R	X	K	B	E	K
V	A	X	N	X	B	M	W	V	C	X
O	P	P	O	R	T	U	N	I	T	Y
Z	E	W	K	H	T	Q	N	X	M	H

Across

1. It doesn't _____ which way you do it.
2. They are both beginners. They are at the same _____level_____ .
3. This new job offer is a great _____ for her.
4. Rose got her hair cut, but her husband didn't _____ .
5. Don't look! Close your eyes and _____ them with your hands.
6. You _____ and I'll follow.

Down

1. How did the man _____ from prison?
2. The president has a great deal of _____ .
3. Helen has a guitar _____ every Tuesday at 5:30.
4. Max is working on a _____ for his science class.

BUILDING DICTIONARY SKILLS

Finding Words in the Dictionary, Part 2

 Sometimes it is easy to find the word you are looking for in the dictionary. For example, look at *suddenly* below. It follows *sudden*. Each word has its own entry.

> **sud•den** /'sʌdn/ *adj* **1** done or happening quickly or in a way you did not expect: *We've had a* **sudden change** *of plans.* | *Don't make any sudden moves around the animals.* **2 all of a sudden** suddenly: *All of a sudden, the lights went out.* —**suddenness** n. [U]
>
> **sud•den•ly** /'sʌdnli/ *adv* quickly and in a way you did not expect: *She suddenly realized what she'd done.* | *Smith died suddenly of a heart attack.*

 Sometimes a word does not have its own entry. For example, look at *bravely* below.

> **brave¹** /breɪv/ *adj* dealing with danger, pain, or difficult situations with courage ANT **cowardly**: *brave soldiers* | *her brave fight against cancer* —**bravely** *adv*

Bravely is an adverb. An adverb ending in *-ly* can often be found at the end of the dictionary entry for the related adjective.

 Phrasal verbs do not usually have their own entries in the dictionary. They are part of the entry for the verb.

Look at this entry for the verb *deal*. Circle the two phrasal verbs.

> **deal²** *v* (past tense and past participle **dealt** /dɛlt/) [I,T] **1** *also* **deal out** to give out playing cards to players in a game: *It's my* **turn to deal**. **2** to buy and sell illegal drugs: *He was arrested for dealing heroin.* **3 deal a blow (to sb/sth)** to harm someone or something: *The ban dealt a severe blow to local tourism.*
>
> **deal in** sth *phr. v* to buy and sell a particular product: *a business dealing in medical equipment*
>
> **deal with** sb/sth *phr. v* **1** to do what is neccessary, especially in order to solve a problem: *Who's dealing with the new account?* **2** to succeed in controlling your feelings and being patient in a difficult situation: *I can't deal with any more crying children today.* **3** to do business with someone: *We've been dealing with their company for ten years.* **4** to be about a particular subject: *a book dealing with 20th-century art*

Vocabulary Self-Test 1

Circle the letter of the word or phrase that best completes each sentence.

Example:

Thousands of people were in the streets to _____ in the celebration.

  a. explain   **b.** pick up   **c.** take part   **d.** discover

1. Chris works for an airline and _____ fly for free.

  a. affords   **b.** explains   **c.** joins   **d.** gets to

2. You can do what you want. It's your _____.

  a. choice   **b.** fear   **c.** root   **d.** shock

3. There have already been a lot of problems, and _____ there will be more.

  a. no doubt   **b.** rather   **c.** no longer   **d.** forward

4. The movie was so _____ that Matt fell asleep.

  a. popular   **b.** professional   **c.** boring   **d.** total

5. How long will it take for this letter to _____ Australia?

  a. accept   **b.** notice   **c.** quit   **d.** reach

6. You close your eyes while we _____. Then you try to find us.

  a. melt   **b.** hide   **c.** expect   **d.** matter

7. I'd like to go out and do something this evening, but I have nothing _____ in mind.

  a. specific   **b.** bored   **c.** alike   **d.** bright

8. After failing two tests, David was in _____ of failing the course.

  a. value   **b.** opportunity   **c.** memory   **d.** danger

9. Your baby is growing fast! How much does she _____?
   a. lead   **b.** weigh   **c.** prepare   **d.** find

10. The teacher isn't here _____. He's going to be a few minutes late.
   a. yet   **b.** against   **c.** except   **d.** wise

11. I have to _____ what's wrong with my computer.
   a. come out   **b.** figure out   **c.** turn out   **d.** go on

12. I'm interested in travel to other countries to learn about their languages and _____.
   a. magic   **b.** levels   **c.** basis   **d.** cultures

13. *Exciting* is the _____ of *boring*.
   a. researcher   **b.** difficulty   **c.** opposite   **d.** variety

14. Jan _____ the name of the company, but I can't remember it.
   a. mentioned   **b.** faced   **c.** disappeared   **d.** rushed

15. The _____ U.S. family in the 1950s had four children.
   a. average   **b.** natural   **c.** brave   **d.** polite

16. Many _____ of the city are not safe for people out walking at night.
   a. areas   **b.** bells   **c.** toys   **d.** members

17. _____ I don't know much about it, I think I'd like to see that movie.
   a. Once   **b.** Although   **c.** In general   **d.** After all

18. He's never had this problem before, and he doesn't know how to _____ it.
   a. turn into   **b.** produce   c. encourage   **d.** deal with

19. The police officer kept his dog under _____ at all times.
   a. attack   **b.** offer   **c.** control   **d.** challenge

20. That young singer has so much _____ that she's sure to become a star.
   a. career   **b.** talent   **c.** tax   **d.** marriage

21. Only one part of the government has the _____ to make new laws.

    a. project   **b.** seed   **c.** enemy   **d.** power

22. Please speak up! We can _____ hear you.

    a. hardly   **b.** however   **c.** suddenly   **d.** a great deal

23. Let's go inside. I think it _____ rain.

    a. shares   **b.** is about to   **c.** manages   **d.** escapes

24. What's the _____ between the old plan and the new one?

    a. couple   **b.** energy   **c.** difference   **d.** lesson

25. Before you start painting, _____ the floor with something to protect it.

    a. cover   **b.** stare   **c.** serve   **d.** consider

26. Pietro has visited _____ every country in South America.

    a. lonely   **b.** nearly   **c.** highly   **d.** naturally

27. I am not _____ of any problems with the machine.

    a. amazing   **b.** disappointed   **c.** aware   **d.** comfortable

28. It was very _____ of her to say such nice things.

    a. terrible   **b.** awful   **c.** dusty   **d.** kind

See the Answer Key on page 239.

A Dentist? Oh, No!

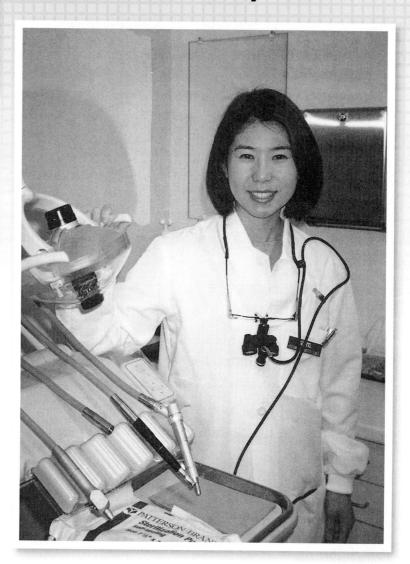

Dr. Kazumi Funamoto, dentist

GETTING READY TO READ

Talk with a partner or in a small group.

1. How often do you go to the dentist?
2. How do you feel about going to the dentist?
3. How many years of schooling does a dentist need?
4. Is being a dentist a good job? Tell why or why not.

READING

Look at the pictures, words, and definitions next to the reading. Then read without stopping. Don't worry about new words. Don't stop to use a dictionary. Just keep reading!

A Dentist? Oh, No!

1 When people ask Kazumi Funamoto, "**What do you do?**" she answers, "I'm a dentist." Then she watches for the look on their faces. The same thing almost always happens. She can see that they are saying to themselves, "A dentist? Oh, no!" She understands how they feel. They are thinking about **needles** and drills[1] and pain.

2 Kazumi does not want her patients to be afraid, so she takes time to talk to them and ease[2] their fears. She tells them, "It's going to be OK. I'm going to be as **gentle** as I can. I don't like pain myself!" She always explains what she is going to do and helps her patients feel **calm** and **relaxed**.

3 When she was a child, Kazumi did not like going to the dentist, and she never expected to become one herself. She used to think about becoming an interpreter[3] because she was interested in other languages and she liked talking to people from other countries. Although Kazumi chose a different career, **communication** is still a big part of her job. She needs to talk with her patients, and she needs to tell her dental assistant[4] what to do. It is important that they understand each other well.

4 Growing up, Kazumi talked about careers with her aunt. She says, "My aunt was a medical technician,[5] and she had a big **influence** on me." This aunt sometimes took Kazumi to work with her. Kazumi liked being in the **lab**, where she could watch and listen to doctors and technicians at work.

5 In college, Kazumi had to get braces[6] on her teeth. "That was no fun," she says, "but the results were wonderful." Then she started to think about becoming a dentist. To learn what the job was like, she spent some time helping in a dentist's office. This experience helped her **make up her mind** to go to dental school after college.

[1] a dentist's *drill*

[2] *ease* = make (a problem) smaller or not so bad

[3] an *interpreter* = a person who repeats someone's words in another language

[4] a *dental assistant* = a worker who helps a dentist

[5] a *medical technician* = a worker who knows how to use machines or do tests that help doctors

[6] *braces*

(continued)

6   Today, Kazumi feels great about her career. When asked, she gives three reasons why she is glad to be a dentist. **First of all**, she knows that she makes her mother happy. Her mother is glad that Kazumi can **support** herself. She told her daughter, "You won't have to depend on a husband. Good for you!"[7] Second, Kazumi likes working with her hands. A dentist needs a gentle touch and great control of very small **movements**. "I think I have good hands for this kind of work," she says. Finally, she enjoys learning new things. She says, "I'm learning from experience and from talking with my boss." At the end of the day, she takes the opportunity to talk to him about difficult **cases**. She asks him questions about problems that **come up** with her patients' teeth, and he **suggests** what to do. Kazumi says, "I feel like I'm growing each and every day."

[7] *Good for you!* = said to show you are happy about something that someone did

Quick Comprehension Check

Read these sentences. Circle T (true) or F (false).

1. All her life, Kazumi Funamoto wanted to be a dentist.   T   F

2. She's not interested in talking to her patients.   T   F

3. She used to go to work with her aunt.   T   F

4. Kazumi's mother is happy that Kazumi is a dentist.   T   F

5. Kazumi works alone.   T   F

6. She is happy to be a dentist.   T   F

EXPLORING VOCABULARY

Thinking about the Target Vocabulary

A Find the six nouns and three adjectives in **bold** in "A Dentist? Oh, No!"
Add them to the chart. Write them in the order they appear in the
reading. Use the singular form of any plural noun.

	Nouns	Verbs	Adjectives	Other
1				What do you do?
2				
3				
4				
5		make up your mind		
6				first of all
		support		
		come up		
		suggest		

B Which words are new to you? Circle them in the chart. Then find the
words in the reading. Look at the context. Can you guess the meaning?

Using the Target Vocabulary

 These sentences are about the reading. Complete them with the words and phrases in the box.

case	gentle	movements	support
come up	influence	relaxed	
first of all	make up her mind	suggesting	

1. Kazumi tells her patients, "I'm going to be as _____ as I can." This means she will be very careful in the way she touches them. She will use a light touch.

2. She doesn't want her patients to be nervous. She wants them to feel _____.

3. Kazumi learned from her aunt while she was growing up. Her aunt had a big _____ on her.

4. After college, Kazumi needed to decide on a career. She needed to _____.

5. Kazumi gives a list of reasons why she feels good about her choice of career. You can introduce a list with the phrase "_____."

6. As a dentist, she makes enough money to live. She can _____ herself.

7. When Kazumi's hands are in a patient's mouth, she needs to move them carefully. She has to use very small _____.

8. Kazumi talks with her boss when she has a difficult _____. In this sentence, the word means a patient's problem.

9. "Problems that _____" are problems that happen, often suddenly, when someone may not be ready for them.

10. When Kazumi explains a problem to her boss, he helps by _____ what she can or should do.

These sentences use the target words and phrases **in new contexts.** Complete them with the words and phrases in the box.

came up	gentle	movements	support
case	influence	relaxed	
first of all	made up my mind	suggested	

1. The doctor tested the _____ of my eyes: up, down, left, and right.

2. They work so they can _____ themselves and their families.

3. They're lying on the beach listening to music. They look very

   _____.

4. Henry tasted the soup and _____ adding more salt.

5. Do you think the new president will have a good _____ on the country?

6. When you have a bad _____ of the flu, you should stay in bed.

7. It was hard to choose which shoes to buy, but finally, I

   _____.

8. He planned to leave work early, but something _____, so he couldn't.

9. Be careful with the baby! You must be _____ with babies.

10. I can think of several reasons not to buy a motorbike.

    _____, they're dangerous.

Read these sentences. Match the boldfaced target words and phrases with their definitions.

a. A family needs good **communication**. Family members have to talk to each other.

b. You work for the college, right? **What do you do?** Do you teach?

c. Police officers and firefighters must stay **calm** so that they can think clearly.

d. A doctor uses a **needle** to give someone a shot of medicine or a drug.

e. We are waiting for test results to come back from the **lab**.

Target Words and Phrases	Definitions
1. _____	= a workplace for scientists and technicians doing research (short for *laboratory*)
2. _____	= giving and getting information (by speaking, writing, and so on)
3. _____	= What is your job?
4. _____	= relaxed, not angry or nervous
5. _____	= a very thin piece of steel

A syringe with a needle

A sewing needle

Building on the Vocabulary: Word Grammar

The verb *suggest* can be used in several ways. Here are three of them:

(a) *suggest* + noun: *She **suggested lunch** at Antonio's.*

(b) *suggest* + *-ing* verb: *I'd **suggest talking** to a lawyer.*

(c) *suggest* + how/where/what/etc.: *He **suggested who** to call for information.*

A Read these statements with *suggest* and look at the three uses of *suggest* in the box. Mark each statement *a*, *b*, or *c*.

1. Doctors suggest getting regular exercise. ____

2. Ann suggested dinner and a movie. ____

3. Can you suggest how to fix it? ____

4. I described the problem, and she suggested what to do. ____

5. I'd suggest asking your professor. ____

6. Carl suggested a walk in the park. ____

B Write two sentences with *suggest*.

1. _____

2. _____

DEVELOPING YOUR SKILLS

Scanning

Read these statements about "A Dentist? Oh, No!" Scan the reading for the information you need to complete them.

1. Kazumi promises her patients that she will be _____.

2. Kazumi also thought about a career as an _____.

3. Communication is important in her work. She needs to talk with _____ and _____.

4. Two experiences helped Kazumi decide on a career as a dentist:

   first, _____;

   then, _____.

5. Kazumi gives three reasons for liking her work:

   a. _____,

   b. _____, and

   c. _____.

The Main Idea

 What is the main idea of the reading in this chapter? Check your answer.

- ☐ **1.** Kazumi Funamoto knows that people don't like to go to the dentist.

- ☐ **2.** A dentist needs to have good hands and a gentle touch to help patients stay calm.

- ☐ **3.** Kazumi Funamoto didn't always expect to be a dentist, but now she is happy in that career.

 What is the main idea of paragraph 6? Write your answer.

_____

Discussion

Talk about these questions with a partner or in a small group.

1. What happens when Kazumi meets someone and says, "I'm a dentist"?

2. How does she feel about her career choice? Why?

3. How did Kazumi's aunt have an influence on her?

4. Who had the biggest influence on you when you were a child? Who has an influence on you now?

5. Name five to ten jobs in which a person works with his or her hands. Would you like any of these jobs? Explain.

Using New Words

Work with a partner. Choose five target words or phrases from the chart on page 99. On a piece of paper, use each word or phrase in a sentence.

Writing

Write a paragraph about a time when you had to make an important decision. Answer these questions:

- What did you decide? Why?

- Did anyone have an influence on your decision?

- How do you feel about your decision now?

Example:

One of my biggest decisions in life was to come to the United States with my family. My husband and I made this decision together. We wanted to do it for our children. They have more opportunities here for education and careers. It wasn't easy because we had no other family here. Now I am glad we came, but of course I miss my family and friends back home.

CHAPTER 10

A Cool Job

Charles Lane

GETTING READY TO READ

Talk in a small group or with the whole class.

1. What video games can you name?

2. Do you ever play video games? Tell why or why not.

3. Charles Lane works for a video game company. He started by working as a video game tester. Does this sound like a good job for you or anyone you know? Tell why or why not.

READING

Look at the picture, words, and definitions next to the reading. Then read without stopping.

A Cool Job

1   Charles Lane loves playing games, all kinds of games. He has loved games all his life. He has always been interested in computers, too. Today, his love of games and his interest in computers come together in his work for a company that makes video games.

2   Charles did not really plan on this career. "It all started **by accident**," he says. "A friend of a friend worked for a video game company. He knew how much I loved games, and he told me about a job. It **sounded** like fun." It was a job as a video game tester.

3   When a video game company is **developing** a new game, they give it to testers. Testers play the game to look for bugs in it. The word *bug* usually means an **insect**, but it can also mean a problem in a computer **program**. "For example," says Charles, "you're playing a war game, and you're flying a plane. You drop a bomb[1] on a building, but nothing happens—the building is still standing. The bomb didn't work, so you know there's a bug." It is the tester's responsibility to find the bugs in a game so that the company can fix them before selling the game to the public.[2]

[1] a *bomb*

4   Video game testers need to have good computer skills and a basic understanding of how computers work. They have to be able to install[3] new **hardware** and **software** as needed. Charles did not have all the computer skills the company was looking for when he went to his job **interview**, so he was rather nervous. However, the interviewer said, "That's OK. We can teach someone to use a computer, but we can't teach someone to love games."

[2] *the public* = all the people (in a city, country, etc.)

[3] *install* = put in place and make ready to use

5   Testers must have strong communication skills, too. They have to write very clear reports on the bugs they find and describe **exactly** what is wrong in a game. Oral[4] communication skills are also important because testers are part of a team. Every

[4] *oral* = spoken, not written

(continued)

day, they talk with other people on the team, such as the game designers[5] and programmers.[6] They all have to work together to **make sure** their games are fun and easy to use.

6   In his first job as a tester, Charles sometimes had to check **certain** parts of a game. At other times, he just started at the beginning and played the **entire** game, looking for bugs. He tried to imagine all the things that a player at home might do in a game. He played hour after hour, day after day, always **paying attention** to details. Did he ever get tired of playing? "You bet!"[7] says Charles. "After sixty hours of testing in a week, you do not want to play games when you get home."

7   Charles spent three years as a video game tester. Now he is a video game **producer**, managing a team that is developing a new game. He really enjoys his work. Charles says, "It's a great **field** to be in."

[5] *designers* = people who plan what things will look like and how they will work

[6] *programmers* = people who write the instructions that make computers do their jobs

[7] *You bet!* = (informal) a strong *yes*

Quick Comprehension Check

Read these sentences. Circle T (true) or F (false).

1. Charles always planned to work for a video game company.   T   F

2. Testers check new games to look for any problems.   T   F

3. Testers need to know something about computers.   T   F

4. Testers don't need to be good writers or speakers.   T   F

5. It usually takes a team of people to make a new video game.   T   F

6. Charles wants to change to a different career.   T   F

EXPLORING VOCABULARY

Thinking about the Target Vocabulary

 A Find the seven nouns in **bold** in "A Cool Job." Add them to the chart. Use the singular form of any plural noun.

	Nouns	Verbs	Adjectives	Other
2				by accident
		sound		
3		develop		
4				
5				exactly
		make sure		
6			certain	
			entire	
		pay attention		
7				

B Which words are new to you? Circle them in the chart. Then find the words in the reading. Look at the context. Can you guess the meaning?

Using the Target Vocabulary

 These sentences are about the reading. Complete them with the words and phrases in the box.

| by accident | develop | field | make sure | producer |
| certain | exactly | interview | pay attention | sounded |

1. Charles's career in video games started _____. He didn't plan on it.

2. Charles listened to his friend describe the job of video game tester. The job _____ like fun.

3. Video game companies _____ new games. A team of people works on a game for a long time to make it a success.

4. Charles was invited to come in and talk to someone about a job at the company. He had an _____.

5. Testers have to describe a bug _____. They have to tell every little thing about it.

6. Video game developers want their games to work well. They want to _____ there are no problems.

7. Sometimes Charles didn't test every part of a game. He tested _____ parts only.

8. You can't think about other things when you test a game. You have to _____ to the game.

9. Charles is now a video game _____. This is a person who is responsible for the people developing a product.

10. Charles likes the video game business. He says it is a great _____ to work in.

B These sentences use the target words and phrases **in new contexts.** Complete them with the words and phrases in the box.

by accident	developing	field	make sure	producer
certain	exactly	interviews	paying attention	sounds

1. Many people like to read about or watch _____ with movie stars.

2. Please _____ the windows are closed. I think it's about to rain.

3. I didn't expect to see her. We met _____.

4. A movie _____ finds the money to pay people to make a film.

5. Your idea _____ interesting. Tell me more.

6. The accident happened because the driver wasn't _____.

7. Scientists are _____ new drugs to fight AIDS.

8. What time is it? It is _____ 4:31.

9. He doesn't work every day, only _____ days.

10. Teachers work in the _____ of education.

C Read each definition and look at the paragraph number. Look back at the reading on pages 107–108 to find the **boldfaced** word to match the definition. Copy it in the chart.

Definition	Paragraph	Target Word
1. a set of instructions given to a computer to make it do a certain job	3	
2. a small creature (such as an ant or a fly) with six legs	3	
3. a set of programs to tell a computer what to do	4	
4. computer machinery and equipment	4	
5. whole or complete	6	

Building on the Vocabulary: Studying Collocations

Collocations are words that we often put together. Some words can go together and some cannot. For example, we can say, *He **pays** attention in class*, but we can't say, *He **gives** attention in class*.

Other verb + noun pairs are
  do + a job, the dishes, the laundry, homework, business
  make + a mistake, money, a choice, a phone call, a decision
  take + a chance, lessons, a picture, a course, time

Which verb goes with the boldfaced noun? Cross out the wrong verb.

1. The teacher told them to (pay / give) **attention**.
2. He (did / made) all his **homework**.
3. Has she (taken / made) a **decision**?
4. Do you mind if I (do / make) a **phone call**?
5. George is (taking / doing) guitar **lessons**.
6. The company (makes / does) a lot of **business** in South America.
7. I plan to (take / do) a math **course**.
8. She (makes / takes) good **money** at her job.

DEVELOPING YOUR SKILLS

Reading for Details

Are these statements about the reading true or false? If the reading doesn't give the information, check (✓) It doesn't say.

	True	False	It doesn't say.
1. Charles loved games when he was a child.	☐	☐	☐
2. He was interested in computers when he was a boy.	☐	☐	☐
3. He got his first job with a video game company after reading about the job in the newspaper.	☐	☐	☐
4. Video game testers need writing skills.	☐	☐	☐
5. Charles had an interview for his first job as a tester.	☐	☐	☐
6. He finished college before becoming a tester.	☐	☐	☐
7. Video game testers look for bugs in games.	☐	☐	☐
8. They sometimes work more than fifty hours a week.	☐	☐	☐
9. Testers usually make a lot of money.	☐	☐	☐
10. Charles still works as a video game tester.	☐	☐	☐

Definitions

Sometimes a reading gives you a definition of a new word or phrase.
A definition often follows this pattern:

A [＿＿＿] is a [＿＿＿] who/that [＿＿＿]

- A programmer is a person who writes computer software.
- A computer is an electronic machine that stores information and lets you work with it.

Use information from the reading to write definitions of the words in parentheses. Follow the pattern:

A [＿＿＿＿] is a [＿＿＿＿] who [＿＿＿＿]

1. (video game tester) _____

   _____

2. (video game producer) _____

   _____

Summarizing

Write a summary of "A Cool Job." Write it as a paragraph. Include the answers to these questions:

- What field does Charles Lane work in?
- What was his first job in the field?
- What do video game testers do?
- What skills and interests are important for testers?
- What does Charles do today?
- How does he feel about his work?

  If you wish, you can begin: *Charles Lane is in the business of developing video games. His first job . . .*

Discussion

Talk about the questions in a small group or with the class.

1. How did Charles Lane get his first job with a video game company?
2. Some people say, "When you are looking for a job, it's *who* you know—not *what* you know—that matters." What does this statement mean? Do you agree with it? Why or why not?
3. Why do video game testers need strong communication skills? What other jobs need these skills? Which of these jobs do you think are good jobs? Why?

Using New Words

Work with a partner. Choose five target words or phrases from the chart on page 111. On a piece of paper, use each word or phrase in a sentence.

Writing

Write a paragraph about your first job. Maybe it was a job you had two months ago—or twenty years ago. Where did you work, what did you do, and how did you feel about this job? Or maybe your first job is still in your future: When will you get a job, and what would you like to do?

Example:

My first job was in a supermarket when I was sixteen years old. I worked there as a cashier. When I started, I didn't like the job because I didn't know anything about cash registers. I felt stupid. When the store was busy and there were a lot of customers in line, I felt a lot of stress. But day by day, I learned, and now I know everything about using a cash register.

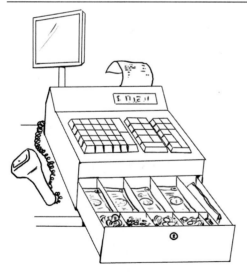

CHAPTER 11

Ready for Action

A crew of firefighters

GETTING READY TO READ

Talk with a partner or in a small group.

1. Look at the photo. What kind of firefighters do you think these are? What are they doing?

2. Do you carry your books in a backpack?[1] If so, how much does it weigh?

3. How long would it take you to hike[2] 3 miles? (That would be almost 5 kilometers.) What about hiking 3 miles with a 45-pound backpack? (That would weigh about 20 kilograms.)

[1] a *backpack*

[2] *hike* = take a long walk in the country, in the mountains, etc.

READING

Look at the pictures, words, and definitions next to the reading. Then read without stopping.

Ready for Action

1   When most people leave for work, they know exactly where they are going. They usually know what time they will get home, too. That is not true for Brandon Middleton. He never knows for sure where he is going or when he will get back. He might **end up** working for eight hours, or ten, or sixteen. Maybe he will not even get home that same week. But that is fine with him. It is all part of being a firefighter for the U.S. Forest Service.

2   Fighting **forest** fires is dangerous work. It can also be very exciting. Imagine being out in a forest, far from any city or town. Maybe you are a smoke jumper and you jumped out of a plane to get there. You are on your way to fight a fire, and the air is heavy with the smoke from the burning trees. As you get closer, the sound of the fire fills your ears like the sound of a train rushing **toward** you. You know that ahead of you is the fire. It is like a monster[1] that you and your team must **destroy**.

3   Is being a firefighter always exciting? Brandon says no. **As a matter of fact**, the first thing he will tell you about the job is, "It's all about **patience**." He and his crew[2] spend a lot of time waiting and a lot of time getting ready. Each one is responsible for his or her own equipment.[3] They have to make sure their **tools** are **sharp**, and they need to have all the right clothes, such as a helmet,[4] **leather** boots, and fire-resistant[5] pants and shirts. Each firefighter will carry a backpack that weighs 25–45 pounds (12–20 kilograms). Firefighters have to be ready to move quickly because they never know when the phone will ring.

4   Three years ago, Brandon was a college student looking for work for the summer. His mother told him that the Forest Service had some jobs **available**. Brandon loves forests and being **outdoors**, so he decided to **apply** for a job as a firefighter. He ended up not going back to college that fall.

5   Brandon had to pass a test for the job. He had to do a 3-mile hike with a 45-pound pack on his back, and he had to do it in

[1] a *monster*

[2] a *crew* = a team of workers

[3] *equipment* = things needed to do a job, play a sport, etc.

[4] a *helmet*

[5] *fire-resistant* = hard to burn

(continued)

less than 45 minutes. Then he needed **training**, so he went to fire school. There he started to learn about things like using firefighting tools, watching the weather, and staying safe. "But fire school is only one week. The real training is on the job," he says. "That is where all the learning happens—out in the forest. You have to trust the people with more experience, and you learn for yourself as you see more fire."

6   What is next for Brandon? He is thinking about applying for a job on a Hotshot crew. The name *Hotshot* **refers** to working in the hottest area of a forest fire, but *hotshot* also means a person who is highly skilled and very confident. Hotshot crews go to all the big fires, and they get the most difficult jobs to do. During the fire **season**, they have to be available 24 hours a day, seven days a week. Not everyone could do this kind of work, and not everyone would want to. "But if this is what you like to do," says Brandon, "you'd love it."

Quick Comprehension Check

Read these sentences. Circle T (true) or F (false).

1. Brandon Middleton loves his work.   T   F

2. He does not work the same hours every day.   T   F

3. Being a firefighter is always exciting.   T   F

4. Firefighters have to carry heavy backpacks.   T   F

5. Brandon learned how to fight fires in college.   T   F

6. He is planning to return to college soon.   T   F

EXPLORING VOCABULARY

Thinking about the Target Vocabulary

 **Find the four verbs and two adjectives in bold in "Ready for Action."
Add them to the chart. Use the base form of each verb.**

	Nouns	Verbs	Adjectives	Other
1				
2	forest			
				toward
3				as a matter of fact
	patience			
	tool			
	leather			
4				
				outdoors
5	training			
6				
	season			

B **Which words are new to you? Circle them in the chart. Then find the
words in the reading. Look at the context. Can you guess the meaning?**

Using the Target Vocabulary

(A) **These sentences are about the reading. What is the meaning of each boldfaced word or phrase? Circle a, b, or c.**

1. Firefighters like Brandon cannot depend on working eight-hour days. They sometimes **end up** working much longer. *End up* means
   a. make something finish or stop.
   b. like or enjoy something.
   c. have a final result you didn't expect.

2. If a fire is moving **toward** you, the sound gets louder. *Toward* means
   a. because of.
   b. away from.
   c. closer to.

3. Being a firefighter isn't always exciting. **As a matter of fact**, it can be very boring. Use *as a matter of fact* to introduce information that is
   a. rather surprising.
   b. totally false.
   c. very encouraging.

4. Brandon is expected to keep his tools **sharp**. *Sharp* means
   a. calm and relaxed.
   b. kind and gentle.
   c. with a thin edge that can cut.

5. Brandon learned that the Forest Service had some jobs **available**. *Available* means
   a. of no value.
   b. ready for someone to take or use.
   c. relating to communication.

6. Brandon wasn't interested in an office job. He likes to be **outdoors** in the fresh air. *Outdoors* means
   a. at home.
   b. at school.
   c. outside and away from buildings.

7. Brandon **applied for** a job as a firefighter. *Apply for something* means
   a. tell people about it.
   b. ask for it (in writing).
   c. disagree with it.

8. New firefighters get their first **training** at fire school. They continue to learn on the job. *Training* means
   a. traveling by train.
   b. trying to get a job.
   c. learning the skills for a job.

9. The word *Hotshot* **refers to** a certain kind of firefighter. *Refers to* means

   a. is about or means.   **b.** comes from.   **c.** is the opposite of.

10. Firefighters work hardest during the fire **season**. *Season* means

   a. the time of year   **b.** a place for   **c.** an interview
   when something   learning to do   for a job.
   happens.   something.

B These sentences use the target words and phrases **in new contexts.** Complete them with the words and phrases in the box.

apply	available	outdoors	seasons	toward
as a matter of fact	ended up	refers to	sharp	training

1. Be careful with that _____ knife!

2. The question "What do you do?" _____ the kind of work you do.

3. She finally made up her mind to leave the company, and she began to _____ for other jobs.

4. Doctors study for many years. They need a lot of _____.

5. The hotel is full. There are no more rooms _____.

6. Canada has four _____: summer, winter, spring, and fall.

7. I tried to install the new software by myself, but I _____ calling Customer Support for help.

8. We wanted to eat _____, but it was raining.

9. You're asking whose responsibility it is? _____, it's yours!

10. She is running _____ him.

Read each definition and look at the paragraph number. Look back at the reading on pages 121–122 to find the boldfaced word to match the definition. Copy it in the chart.

Definition	Paragraph	Target Word
1. a place where many trees cover a large area of land	2	
2. break or hurt something so badly that it cannot continue or be used	2	
3. made of animal skin that has been prepared for use in shoes, belts, etc.	3	
4. the ability to wait for a long time without becoming nervous or angry	3	
5. things that are useful for doing a job	3	

A firefighter may use these *tools:*

an axe   a saw   a shovel

Building on the Vocabulary: Word Grammar

Nouns can modify other nouns. That is, they can act like adjectives, as in:

*Brandon fights **forest fires**.* (fires happening in a forest)

*He wears **leather boots**.* (boots made of leather)

*He spent time at **fire school**.* (a school for learning about fire)

Two nouns can also become a compound noun, as in *firefighter* and *backpack*.

A **Circle the nouns that modify other nouns.**

1. Pam works as a (computer) programmer at a (toy) company.

2. The boys are working on their science projects.

3. I planted some flower seeds around my vegetable garden.

4. Some of my childhood memories are amazingly clear.

5. Gail showed her strong communication skills at her job interview.

6. Doctors sometimes wear lab coats.

B **Write three sentences with nouns modifying other nouns. You can use nouns from the boxes or choose your own.**

music		teacher
math	+	lesson
language		class

1. _____

2. _____

3. _____

DEVELOPING YOUR SKILLS

Scanning

Read these questions about "Ready for Action." Scan the reading and write short answers.

1. How many hours does Brandon Middleton work in a day?

   _____

2. What two words describe the work of fighting forest fires?

   _____ and _____

3. Who first told Brandon about jobs with the Forest Service?

   _____

4. What test did he take? _____

5. Where did he learn to fight fires? _____ and

   _____

Definitions

Use information from the reading to write definitions of the words in parentheses. Follow the pattern:

A [ ] is a [ ] who/that [ ]

1. (smoke jumper) _____

_____

2. (Hotshot crew) _____

_____

Reading Between the Lines

You cannot scan the reading for quick answers to these questions. These are inference or opinion questions. To answer them, you must put information from the reading together with what you know or believe. Write complete sentences.

1. Why does the Forest Service give a test to new firefighters? Maybe the Forest Service wants to see how strong the new firefighters are, or maybe the test is to show the new people how hard the job is.

2. Why does Brandon say, "It's all about patience"? _____

_____

_____

3. What is the meaning of "the fire season" in paragraph 6? _____

_____

4. Why do you think Brandon wants to join a Hotshot crew? _____

_____

_____

Discussion

Talk about these questions in a small group.

1. How did Brandon Middleton become a member of the U.S. Forest Service?

2. Why is this a good job for him?

3. Fighting forest fires can be exciting. What other jobs do you think are exciting?

4. What do people in your country think of firefighters?

5. How would you feel if your husband or wife were a firefighter? Why?

Using New Words

Work with a partner. Choose five target words or phrases from the chart on page 119. On a piece of paper, use each word or phrase in a sentence.

Writing

Brandon learned about firefighting from people on the job. He says, "You have to trust the people with more experience." Write a paragraph about learning from other people and their experience. You can write about:

• a time when you learned something this way, or

• using your own experience to teach someone else.

Examples:

When I learned to drive, I learned from my . . .

I have a younger sister, and I want her to learn from my experience so that she does not . . .

CHAPTER 12

Life Is Full of Surprises

Mahmoud Arani in the classroom

GETTING READY TO READ

Talk in a small group or with the whole class.

1. Mahmoud Arani is from Iran. Tell what you know about Iran.
2. Many people leave their countries to study or to work. List some reasons why people do this.

READING

Look at the words and definitions next to the reading. Then read without stopping.

Life Is Full of Surprises

1   Mahmoud Arani is a **professor** at a small U.S. college. He did not expect to end up in the United States, and he did not expect to teach. He grew up in Iran, and he planned to be a doctor. However, as people say, life is full of surprises.

2   Mahmoud was born in Iran near the city of Tehran. In high school, he was an excellent student—the best in his class—and he was planning on a career in **medicine**. First, he had to take the national university entrance exam.[1] He needed to do well on the exam to **get into** a **medical** school. Out of 50,000 high school students taking the test, only 1,000 would get the chance to study medicine. Mahmoud missed the **score** he needed by a few points, which his teachers found very surprising. He took the test again, and again the news was bad. "I was disappointed," he remembers, "but I said, 'That is my fate.'"[2]

3   Mahmoud was also interested in languages, so he chose to study English. After college, he decided to go to the United States for an **advanced** degree[3] in this **subject**. A few months later, he entered an English as a Second Language (ESL) program. It was in Buffalo, New York, at the state university there. Mahmoud was one of half a million **international** students who entered the United States to study that year, but he **managed to** do something that few others could. In less than two years, he went from studying ESL to teaching it at the same school!

4   While on a visit home from New York, Mahmoud had an interview at a university in Tehran. They offered him a teaching job, and he accepted it. Officials[4] at the university made an agreement with him: Mahmoud would return to Buffalo to finish his degree, and they would give him financial[5] support. After he finished, he would come back to teach. So Mahmoud went back to New York feeling great, believing that his future was **secure**.

(continued)

[1] *the national university entrance exam* = a test all Iranian students had to take to be able to enter college

[2] *fate* = the things that will happen that a person cannot control

[3] *a degree* = what a student gets for completing a program at a college or university

[4] *officials* = people with responsibility and power in an organization or government

[5] *financial* = relating to money

5   Things did not turn out as he expected, however. There was a revolution[6] in Iran, which **caused** great changes in the country. Soon Mahmoud received a letter from his university in Tehran. It said, "We don't need any English teachers." **All of a sudden**, his support was gone, and his future was unclear.

6   Mahmoud decided not to **give up**. He went on working toward his degree, and after much hard work, he reached his goal. Then, after teaching ESL in Buffalo for a while, he accepted a job at Saint Michael's College in Vermont.

7   Things have **worked out** well for Mahmoud. His students at Saint Michael's report that he is an excellent teacher. He is married, and he and his wife, Roya, have two children. Roya, who is also from Iran, is a doctor. Mahmoud is still interested in medicine, too. "I could go to medical school now," he says, "if I had the patience!" He says that he does not plan to make a career change at this **stage** in his life. However, he adds, "I know that life is full of surprises. . . . "

[6] a *revolution* = a time of great and sudden change in a country, often by force

Quick Comprehension Check

Read these sentences. Circle T (true) or F (false).

1. Mahmoud was born and grew up in Iran.   T   F

2. He wanted to study medicine and become a doctor.   T   F

3. He traveled to the United States to study medicine.   T   F

4. He expected to teach at a university in Iran.   T   F

5. The Iranian revolution happened while he was at home in Tehran.   T   F

6. The revolution changed his life.   T   F

EXPLORING VOCABULARY

Thinking about the Target Vocabulary

 A Find the five verbs and four adjectives in **bold** in "Life Is Full of Surprises." Add them to the chart. Use the base form of each verb.

	Nouns	Verbs	Adjectives	Other
1	professor			
2	medicine			
	score			
3				
	subject			
4				
5				
				all of a sudden
6				
7				
	stage			

B Which words are new to you? Circle them in the chart. Then find the words in the reading. Look at the context. Can you guess the meaning?

Using the Target Vocabulary

 These sentences are about the reading. Complete them with the words and phrases in the box.

all of a sudden	get into	international	medicine	subject
caused	give up	managed to	stage	worked out

1. Mahmoud wanted to study _____ so that he could become a doctor.

2. Mahmoud had to do well on a test to _____ medical school. The test decided which students could enter the school.

3. In college, he took many English courses. English was the _____ that he studied most.

4. In the year that Mahmoud entered the United States to study, 500,000 other _____ students did the same. These were students from countries around the world.

5. Mahmoud was able to do something unusual. He _____ do something that few international students could do.

6. Great changes happened in Iran because of the revolution. The revolution _____ these changes.

7. Mahmoud wasn't expecting to lose his financial support. It happened _____.

8. It was hard for Mahmoud to keep going, but he didn't _____. He never stopped trying.

9. Mahmoud has ended up with a good life. Things have _____ well for him.

10. At one time, Mahmoud wanted to become a doctor. But at this _____ of his life, he is happy as a professor.

These sentences use the target words and phrases **in new contexts.** Complete them with the words and phrases in the box.

all of a sudden	gave up	international	medicine	subjects
caused	get into	managed to	stages	work out

1. Parts of the ocean that do not belong to any one country are called _____ waters.
2. Children go through different _____ as they grow.
3. College students can take courses in math, history, education, and many other _____.
4. There was an accident on the road ahead of us. It _____ traffic problems.
5. I kept trying to call you, but your phone was always busy, so finally I _____.
6. You need good grades if you want to _____ a good college.
7. I couldn't open the door, but I _____ get in through a window.
8. Doctors, dentists, and nurses all work in the field of _____.
9. I have high hopes for this project. I think everything will _____ fine in the end.
10. We were eating dinner when _____, the lights went out.

C Read these sentences. Match the **boldfaced** target words with their definitions on page 132.

a. I didn't get a good **score** on the test, so I was disappointed.
b. The **professor** is available to talk with students during her office hours.
c. He can relax and stop worrying about money. He has a **secure** job now.
d. You can get good **medical** care at that hospital.
e. We are both studying Spanish, but I'm a beginner and he's in an **advanced** class.

Target Words	Definitions
1. _____	= a teacher at a college or university
2. _____	= not expected to change or be in any danger
3. _____	= relating to a school subject at a difficult level
4. _____	= relating to medicine and the care of people who are sick or hurt
5. _____	= the number of points someone gets on a test or in a game

Building on the Vocabulary: Studying Collocations

Some adjectives are often followed by a certain **preposition**.
Prepositions are words like *in*, *at*, *by*, and *about*. Here are some
examples of adjective + preposition combinations:

> *aware + of*
> *bored + with*
> *disappointed + with/in*
> *gentle + with*
> *interested + in*
> *kind + to*
> *polite + to*

Complete the sentences. Add the preposition that goes with the adjective.

1. You must be gentle _____ small children.
2. The president wasn't aware _____ the true situation.
3. He was angry, but he still managed to be polite _____ them.
4. Do you get bored _____ your job?
5. We were disappointed _____ the results.
6. I'm interested _____ medicine.
7. His neighbors were very kind _____ him after his wife died.

DEVELOPING YOUR SKILLS

Reading for Details

Are these statements about the reading true or false? If the reading doesn't give the information, check (✓) *It doesn't say.*

		True	False	It doesn't say.
1.	Mahmoud was born in Iran.	☐	☐	☐
2.	He studied English in college.	☐	☐	☐
3.	He went to the United States to look for a job.	☐	☐	☐
4.	Mahmoud's visit to Iran lasted for six months.	☐	☐	☐
5.	The revolution in Iran happened while he was there.	☐	☐	☐
6.	He received a degree from the state university in Buffalo, New York.	☐	☐	☐
7.	He is a husband and a father.	☐	☐	☐
8.	He and his wife are both professors.	☐	☐	☐
9.	He is now planning to enter medical school.	☐	☐	☐
10.	All of Mahmoud's family is in the United States.	☐	☐	☐

Definitions

Use information from the reading to write definitions of the words in parentheses. Follow the pattern:

A/An [＿＿＿＿] is a [＿＿＿＿] who/that [＿＿＿＿]

1. (international student) ＿＿＿＿＿＿＿＿＿＿＿＿＿＿＿＿＿＿＿

＿＿＿＿＿＿＿＿＿＿＿＿＿＿＿＿＿＿＿＿＿＿＿＿＿

2. (entrance exam) ＿＿＿＿＿＿＿＿＿＿＿＿＿＿＿＿＿＿＿

＿＿＿＿＿＿＿＿＿＿＿＿＿＿＿＿＿＿＿＿＿＿＿＿＿

Cause and Effect

Complete the following sentences with *because* using information from "Life Is Full of Surprises."

1. Mahmoud's grade on the exam surprised his teachers because <u>he was the best sudent in his class, but his score wasn't high enough for medical school</u>.

2. Mahmoud decided to study English because _____.

3. He went to the United States because _____.

4. As an international student, Mahmoud was unusual because _____ _____.

5. He lost the chance to teach in Tehran because _____.

6. He doesn't plan to start medical school now because _____.

Discussion

Talk with your class about these questions.

1. What were two big surprises in Mahmoud's life? How did they change his life?

2. How many people in the class agree that "life is full of surprises"? Are surprises a good thing in life? Why or why not?

3. How many people in the class would like to teach English? What are some reasons why people in the class do and do not want to?

4. How did your teacher become a teacher of English?

Using New Words

Work with a partner. Choose five target words or phrases from the chart on page 129. On a piece of paper, use each word or phrase in a sentence.

Writing

Choose a topic. Write a paragraph.

1. Describe a time in your life when you set a goal and didn't give up. What were you trying to do? What made it hard? How did you reach your goal?

2. Think back to an earlier stage in your life. Write about a time when you wanted something very much. Did you get what you wanted, or were you disappointed? Explain.

REVIEWING VOCABULARY

 A Match these nouns with their definitions. There are two extra words.

field	lab	score	subject
influence	medicine	season	training

1. _____ = the teaching or learning of skills for a certain job

2. _____ = an area of business or professional study

3. _____ = something that someone studies or talks or writes about

4. _____ = a part of the year when certain weather is expected or when something happens most often

5. _____ = the study and the field of caring for people who are sick or hurt

6. _____ = the power to make changes in how someone thinks or how something develops

B Complete these sentences with phrases from the box. There are two extra phrases.

apply for	ended up	give up	manage to	refer to
came up	get into	make sure	pay attention	work out

1. He turned off the TV to _____ to his homework.

2. She had a good interview and _____ getting the job.

3. A problem _____, so I needed some advice.

4. The computer isn't working, but I'm sure Yoko will _____ fix it.

5. Try not to worry. Everything will _____ well in the end.

6. The words *they* and *them* can _____ people or things.

7. Don't _____ ! I know you can do it. Keep trying.

8. You need very good grades to _____ the top universities.

EXPANDING VOCABULARY

Adverbs have many uses. An adverb can modify (or describe) a verb, an adjective, another adverb, or an entire sentence. An adverb can be one word or a phrase.

verb + adverb	She **spoke** calmly. He **answered** me politely.	They **fought** bravely. **Put** the baby **down** gently.
adverb + **adjective**	He looked very **relaxed**. That is exactly **right**.	I'm not entirely **sure**. The class was too **advanced** for me.
adverb + **adverb**	He can sing amazingly **well**.	It turned out rather **badly**.
adverb + **sentence**	All of a sudden, it disappeared into the forest. First of all, make sure you dress well for the interview. As a matter of fact, no—I have *not* made up my mind.	

A Complete the sentences. Use adverbs from the box above. For most sentences, there can be more than one answer.

1. The firefighter _____ entered the burning building.

2. _____, make a list of the things you will need.

3. His experience and mine were _____ different.

4. _____, the car started to make a terrible sound.

5. He asked his questions _____.

6. They are _____ talented dancers.

B **Write two sentences with adverbs from the box on page 137.**

1. _____

2. _____

A PUZZLE

Complete the sentences with words you studied in Chapters 9–12. Write the words in the puzzle.

Across

2. Professors are _____ to talk to students during office hours.

3. She has strong _____ skills.

5. Will the job pay enough for you to _____ yourself?

7. A team of doctors is working on the _____.

10. I love spending time _____.

11. A team of people at the university is _____ some new language programs.

Down

1. Doctors-in-training are called _____ students, or *med students*.

4. Only _____ people will be invited.

5. Joe _____ meeting at 4:00, and we all agreed.

6. Does she have the _____ to be a teacher?

8. We turned _____ the sound.

9. He is taking an _____ math course.

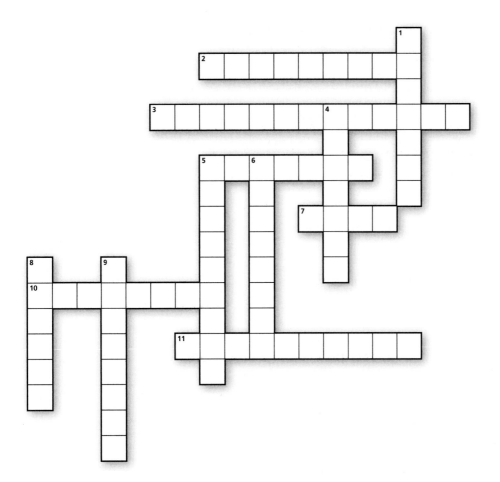

BUILDING DICTIONARY SKILLS

Many words can be more than one part of speech. They may have more than one entry in the dictionary. The dictionary will have a superscript (a small, raised number) after a word to tell you that there is more than one entry.

Many words have more than one meaning. The different meanings are numbered in the dictionary.

Look at the two entries for *cause* and answer the questions below.

> **cause¹** /kɔz/ *n* **1** [C] a person, event, or thing that makes something happen: *What was the* **cause** *of the accident?* **2** [C,U] a reason for doing something or having a particular feeling: *There is* **no** **cause for concern/alarm.** **3** [C] a principle or aim that a group of people support or fight for: *I don't mind giving money if it's* **for a good cause.**
>
> **cause²** *v* [T] to make something happen, especially something bad: *Heavy traffic is causing long delays.* | *We still don't know what* **caused** *the computer* **to** *crash.*

1. Which parts of speech can *cause* be? Circle your answers.

   noun   verb   adjective   adverb

2. How many meanings of *cause* does the dictionary give? _____

B   **Look up these words in your English dictionary. Find out how many parts of speech the dictionary shows for each word. Find out how many meanings it shows. How many are new to you? Complete the chart.**

	Which parts of speech can it be?	How many meanings does it have?	How many are new to you?
Example:* sharp	adj. and adv.	16	
1. calm			
2. secure			
3. sound			
4. stage			

* As shown in the *Longman Dictionary of American English*, fourth edition.

4

IT'S ALL IN YOUR HEAD

Food for Thought

Morning coffee

GETTING READY TO READ

Talk in a small group or with the whole class.

1. How many people in the group drink:

   ____ coffee

   ____ tea

   ____ soda, such as Coke or Pepsi

   ____ energy drinks

2. All the drinks in the list have caffeine.[1] Do you know any other drinks with caffeine?

3. When and why do people like drinks with caffeine?

   [1] *caffeine* = a substance (in coffee, tea, and some other drinks) that helps tired minds wake up

Look at the picture, words, and definitions next to the reading. Then read without stopping. Don't worry about new words. Don't stop to use a dictionary. Just keep reading!

Food for Thought

1   The foods you eat **supply** your body with energy. Your body needs energy to move and even to sleep. One part of your body uses a surprising **amount** of energy. It is surprising because this part of your body is small—only 2–3 percent of your total **weight**—but it uses 20–30 percent of the energy from your food. Can you guess what it is? It is your brain.

2   You already know that drugs **affect** the brain. Did you know that food affects it, too? Different types of food affect the brain in different ways. Sometimes we can feel the changes that food makes in our brains. For example, most people can feel a change almost **immediately** after drinking coffee. It is the caffeine in coffee that affects the brain, making people feel mentally sharper[1] and more awake. After a cup of coffee, a person can think and make decisions more quickly.

[1] *mentally sharper = able to think and understand more quickly*

3   Other foods affect the brain in ways that we cannot see or feel, so we are not aware of them. We do not **realize** how these foods influence us. However, everything we eat matters. Our food affects how smart we are and how well we remember things. It also affects how long we can concentrate.[2] For example, researchers have found that:

[2] *concentrate = think carefully*

1. Eating breakfast makes students do better on tests.

2. Spinach, berries, and other colorful fruits and vegetables help keep older brains from slowing down.

3. Eating large amounts of animal fat (in meat and cheese, for example) makes learning more difficult.

4. Fish really is "brain food." Many people have long believed that eating fish was good for the brain. Now scientists are finding that this is true.

4   For millions of years, the brains of early human beings[3] stayed the same size. They weighed only about 1 pound (400–

[3] *early human beings = the first people who lived*

(continued)

500 grams). Then, during the last million years **or so**, there was a big **increase** in brain size. The human brain grew to about 3 pounds. This increase in brain size **meant** an increase in brain power. With bigger, stronger brains, human beings became smart enough to build boats and invent written languages. They developed forms of music and began to **create** works of art.[4]

5   Some scientists say that the big change in the human brain happened after people started to eat seafood.[5] Seafood **contains** a certain kind of fat, known as omega-3 fat. **According to** these scientists, omega-3 fat caused the increase in brain size. Today, brain scientists in general agree: This fat is still important for healthy brains, and most of us are not getting enough of it.

6   Did you realize that your brain is always changing, **no matter** how old you are? The foods you eat affect how your brain grows, how well you learn, and how well you remember things. Maybe you have never thought about how you **feed** your brain. **Luckily**, it is never too late to start feeding it well.

[4] *works of art* = the things that artists make

[5] *seafood*

Quick Comprehension Check

Read these sentences. Circle T (true) or F (false).

1. Your brain is small but uses a lot of energy.   T   F

2. The foods you eat affect the way your brain works.   T   F

3. When a food causes changes in your brain, you
   can always feel it.   T   F

4. Maybe eating fish helped make the human
   brain bigger.   T   F

5. All kinds of fat are bad for you.   T   F

6. Children's brains grow and change, but adult
   brains don't.   T   F

EXPLORING VOCABULARY

Thinking about the Target Vocabulary

A Find the three nouns and seven verbs in **bold** in "Food for Thought." Add them to the chart. Write them in the order they appear in the reading. Use the singular form of any plural noun and the base form of each verb.

	Nouns	Verbs	Adjectives	Other
1				
2				
				immediately
3				
4				or so
5				
				according to
6				no matter
				luckily

B Which words are new to you? Circle them in the chart. Then find the words in the reading. Look at the context. Can you guess the meaning?

Using the Target Vocabulary

 A **These sentences are about the reading. Complete them with the words and phrases in the box.**

according to	contains	immediately	meant	supplies
affects	create	luckily	realize	weight

1. Food gives us energy. When we eat, food _____ our bodies with energy.

2. Your brain is not very heavy. It is only 2 to 3 percent of your total body _____.

3. Drugs influence, or cause changes in, the brain. Food _____ it, too.

4. Sometimes a drug or food affects the brain quickly and people feel the difference very soon. They feel a change _____.

5. Many people aren't aware that food affects the brain. They don't _____ that this is true.

6. When human brains got bigger, that _____ more brain power. The larger brain led to that result.

7. Early humans invented languages and also began to produce music and art. They started to _____ these things.

8. Some scientists say that eating seafood caused big changes. _____ these scientists, seafood helped the human brain to grow.

9. There is omega-3 fat in seafood. Seafood _____ this kind of fat.

10. Maybe you never thought about eating "brain food" before. _____, it's not too late. That is a good thing.

B These sentences use the target words and phrases **in new contexts.** Complete them with the words and phrases in the box.

according to	contain	immediately	meant	supplies
affects	create	luckily	realize	weight

1. There was a car accident there today. _____, no one was hurt.

2. Fruit is often sold by _____—you pay by the pound or kilogram.

3. There were no surprises in the report. It didn't _____ any new information.

4. The weather often _____ people's travel plans.

5. He needed medical care _____, so we rushed him to the hospital.

6. She was already in bed when I called. I didn't _____ it was so late.

7. The company _____ its workers with all the tools they need.

8. We got a foot of snow, and that _____ that we had no school the next day.

9. I have no more patience with them. They just _____ problems for everyone else.

10. _____ the newspaper, there will be a lot of jobs in that field in the years ahead.

Read each definition and look at the paragraph number. Look back at the reading on pages 143–144 to find the boldfaced word or phrase to match the definition. Copy it in the chart.

Definition	Paragraph	Target Word or Phrase
1. how much of something there is	1	
2. a phrase used when you cannot give an exact number or amount	4	
3. a change to a higher number or larger amount	4	
4. a phrase meaning something is always true or the same, even when you would expect a change	6	
5. give food to	6	

Building on the Vocabulary: Studying Collocations

Remember: Collocations are words that go together. Certain adjectives go with the noun **amount**.

- Use *large* + *amount* but not *big amount*.
- Use *small* + *amount* but not *little amount*.

Use *amount* + *of* + noncount noun (such as *energy*, *time*, *money*, or *work*).

Examples:

He never carries large amounts of money.

I eat chocolate in small amounts.

Write three sentences with *amount*.

1. _____

_____

2. _____

_____

3. _____

_____

DEVELOPING YOUR SKILLS

Scanning

Read these statements about "Food for Thought." Scan the reading for the information you need to complete them. Answers inside quotation marks (" ") must match the words in the reading exactly.

1. The foods you eat give your body _____.

2. The brain makes up only _____ percent of your body's total weight.

3. The brain uses _____ percent of the energy from your food.

4. The _____ in coffee makes people feel more awake.

5. Scientists have found that:
   a. "Eating breakfast _____."
   b. "_____" are good for older brains.
   c. "Eating large amounts of animal fat _____
      _____."
   d. "_____ really is 'brain food.'"

6. Early human brains grew from about _____ to about
   _____.

7. Some scientists say the human brain grew because of the
   _____ in seafood.

8. With bigger, stronger brains, human beings were able to build
   _____, invent _____, and create
   _____.

Thinking about the Main Idea

A **Complete the main idea of "Food for Thought."**

The foods you eat affect how _____.

B What is the main idea of paragraph 1 in "Food for Thought"? Write one or two sentences.

_____

_____

C What is the main idea of paragraph 6 in "Food for Thought"? Write one or two sentences.

_____

_____

Reading Between the Lines

You cannot scan the reading for quick answers to these questions. These are inference or opinion questions. To answer them, you must put information from the reading together with what you know or believe. Write complete sentences.

1. What advice about food does the reading contain for people in

   general? _____

   _____

2. What advice about food does the reading contain for students?

   _____

   _____

3. According to the reading, what do scientists disagree on?

   _____

   _____

Discussion

Talk about these questions in a small group.

1. According to some scientists, what caused a big increase in the size of early human brains? What were people able to do as a result?

2. At what times during the day do you think your brain works best? Why?

3. How much would you change the way you eat to make yourself smarter? What is one thing you would do? What is one thing you would not do?

4. What questions would you like to ask scientists about food and the brain? Make a list.

Using New Words

Work with a partner. Choose five target words or phrases from the chart on page 145. On a piece of paper, use each word or phrase in a sentence.

Writing

Write a paragraph about something you like to eat or drink. When do you usually have it? How does it affect you? Do you think it's good or bad for you? Why?

Your Memory at Work

Trying to remember . . .

GETTING READY TO READ

Talk with a partner or in a small group.

1. Look at the things in the list. Which ones are usually easy for you to remember? Which ones are hard?

people's names	colors	words to songs
people's faces	music	information from classes
numbers	new vocabulary in English	other: _____

2. When you MUST remember something, what do you do? How do you help yourself remember it?

READING

Look at the picture, words, and definitions next to the reading. Then read without stopping.

Your Memory at Work

1   You have two basic types of memory: short-**term** memory and long-term memory. Things you see or hear first enter your short-term memory. Very little of this information then passes on into your long-term memory. Does this mean you have a bad memory? Not at all.

2   Your short-term memory has a certain job to do. Its job is to store information for a few seconds only. You use your short-term memory when you look up a phone number, call it, and then forget it. You remember the number just long enough to use it, and then it disappears from your memory. That is really a good thing. Imagine if your memory held every number, face, and word you ever knew! Your brain would hold a mountain of trivia.[1]

[1] *trivia* = unimportant or useless details

3   Of course, we need to remember some information longer, so it has to pass from short-term to long-term memory. Sometimes we tell ourselves to remember: "OK, don't forget: 555-1212, 555-1212 . . . " But usually, we do not even think about it. Our brain makes the decision for us. It decides to store the information or let it go.

4   The brain seems to make the decision by asking two questions:

1. Does the new information affect our **emotions**? **That is**, does it make us happy, sad, excited, or **upset**?

2. Does the information **concern** something we already know, so our brain can store it with information that is already there?

[2] a *cell* = in any living thing, the smallest part that can live by itself

An answer of "yes" to one or both of these questions sends the new information into long-term memory. That means the brain creates new **connections** among brain cells.[2] These connections form in a **region** of the brain called the *cerebral cortex*.[3] It is the largest part of the brain.

(continued)

[3] the *cerebral cortex*

5   After a piece of information enters your long-term memory, how do you get it back? Sometimes your brain may seem like a deep, dark **closet**. You open the door to look for something— you are sure it is in there somewhere—but you cannot find it. Maybe the information really is not there **anymore**. Information disappears when connections among brain cells become **weak**. They get weak if time passes and the connections are not used. That is why it is good to **review** your **notes** from a **lecture** soon after the class. Do not wait too long to "look in the closet."

6   To keep the memory of something strong, think of it often. For example, look at those lecture notes the next day and the day after that, too. Every time you think about something, the connections in the brain get stronger. Then it is easier to remember the information when you need it.

7   **Unfortunately**, this suggestion **applies** only to certain kinds of things that you try to remember. It will not help when you are trying to remember a name that is on the tip of your tongue. A "tip of the tongue" experience is the feeling that you are about to remember a word but it just will not come out. These experiences are common among older adults, but everyone has them. College students, on average, have one or two a week.

8   This suggestion also will not help you remember something that just never made it[4] from short-term to long-term memory. So you will need some other strategy[5] to help you figure out where you left your keys.

[4] *made it* = managed to arrive

[5] *strategy* = plans and skills used to reach a goal

Quick Comprehension Check

Read these sentences. Circle T (true) or F (false).

1. People have two basic types of memory.   T F

2. Your short-term memory holds information for only a few days.   T F

3. All information should go to your long-term memory.   **T**   **F**

4. We usually remember information that affects how we feel.   **T**   **F**

5. Information in long-term memory will always be there.   **T**   **F**

6. There are things you can do to help your memory.   **T**   **F**

EXPLORING VOCABULARY

Thinking about the Target Vocabulary

 Find the three verbs and two adjectives in **bold** in "Your Memory at Work." Add them to the chart. Use the base form of each verb.

	Nouns	Verbs	Adjectives	Other
1	term			
4	emotion			
				that is
	connection			
	region			
5	closet			
				anymore
	notes*			
	lecture			
7				unfortunately

* Always plural when referring to information a student writes in class.

B   **Which words are new to you? Circle them in the chart. Then find the words in the reading. Look at the context. Can you guess the meaning?**

Using the Target Vocabulary

A   **These sentences are about the reading. What is the meaning of each boldfaced word or phrase? Circle a, b, or c.**

1. Information can affect the emotions. **That is**, it can cause certain feelings in us. Use *that is* to
   a. give more exact information.
   b. take the place of *but*.
   c. introduce a question.

2. It is easier to remember new facts or ideas when they **concern** something we already know. *Concern* means
   a. be about.
   b. destroy.
   c. end up.

3. New **connections** form among brain cells when we learn something new. *Connections* means places
   a. where nothing happens.
   b. where things come together.
   c. where something stops.

4. The cerebral cortex is a **region** of the brain. A region is
   a. a tool.
   b. a season.
   c. an area.

5. Sometimes a fact was in someone's brain, but it's **not** there **anymore**. *Not . . . anymore* means
   a. not . . . now.
   b. not . . . exactly.
   c. not . . . luckily.

6. We forget things when connections among brain cells get **weak**. *Weak* means
   a. sharp.
   b. not strong.
   c. secure.

7. It is a good idea to **review** information from a course before a test. *Review something* means to
   a. mention it.
   b. make it disappear.
   c. read it again and study it.

8. Students are wise to review their **notes** soon after a class. Their notes are
   a. their grades.
   b. information they write down in class.
   c. their favorite music.

9. **Unfortunately**, some things that you can do to help your memory won't help you in every case. Use *unfortunately* to introduce information that is

   a. encouraging.   **b.** amazing.   **c.** disappointing.

10. The suggestions in the reading **apply** at certain times but not at others. When a suggestion, law, or rule applies to people, it

    a. affects or concerns them.   **b.** attacks them.   **c.** surprises them.

B These sentences use the target words and phrases **in new contexts**. Complete them with the words and phrases in the box.

apply	connection	notes	review	unfortunately
concerning	not anymore	region	that is	weak

1. Students often take _____ in class about things they want to remember.

2. Many customers had questions _____ the new software.

3. The sales tax does not _____ to sales of food or medicine.

4. Mike lives in a _____ where they get a lot of snow.

5. _____, Elsa wasn't able to get into the program she wanted.

6. Please _____ your notes from the training and let me know if you have questions.

7. People say, "Money is the root of all evil." _____, the love of money causes many of the world's troubles.

8. Wendy gave up coffee. She used to drink ten cups a day, but _____.

9. Being sick for so long made Jeff lose weight and feel _____.

10. When one fact, idea, or event affects another, we can say there is a _____ between them.

Read each definition and look at the paragraph number. Look back at the reading on pages 153–154 to find the boldfaced word to match the definition. Copy it in the chart.

Definition	Paragraph	Target Word
1. a certain amount of time	1	
2. strong feelings, such as love or hate	4	
3. unhappy and worried	4	
4. an area where people hang clothes or store things (behind a door in a wall)	5	
5. a long talk on one subject, given to a group of people, often students	5	

Building on the Vocabulary: Word Grammar

Some adjectives can be used in more than one way. They can come

- before a noun (a *weak arm*)

OR

- after *be* (*My arm was weak.*)

Other adjectives can come after *be* but cannot come before a noun. We cannot say, for example, *The afraid dog ran away.* The adjectives *alike*, *alive*, *aware*, and *upset* are also not used before nouns.

*The two cars **were** exactly **alike**.*

*Her grandmother **is** still **alive**.*

*He **was aware** of the difficulty.*

*They're **upset** about the news.*

Rewrite these sentences. Use adjectives from the box above.

1. She has a fear of flying. *She is afraid of flying.* _____

2. The two needles are the same. _____

3. Everyone lived after the accident. _____

4. Are you unhappy about the project? _____

5. The manager knows about the increase. _____

DEVELOPING YOUR SKILLS

Understanding Topics of Paragraphs

A **Where is the information about these topics in "Your Memory at Work"? Find each topic in the reading and write the paragraph number.**

__4__ **a.** How the brain deals with new information

____ **b.** Types of memory

____ **c.** Weak connections among brain cells

____ **d.** Building strong connections among brain cells

____ **e.** What short-term memory does

____ **f.** "Tip of the tongue" experiences

____ **g.** Getting information from short-term to long-term memory

B **Write a sentence or two about each topic in Part A, beginning with the topic of the first paragraph and continuing in order. Use information from the reading, but do not copy entire sentences. Use your own words.**

1. The two basic types of memory are called short-term memory and long-term memory.

2. _____

_____

_____

3. _____

_____

_____

4. _____

_____

_____

5. _____

_____

_____

6. _____

_____

_____

7. _____

_____

_____

Definitions

Use information from the reading to write a definition of *cerebral cortex*. Follow the pattern:

The [   ] is the [   ] that [   ]

_____

_____

Summarizing

Complete the summary of "Your Memory at Work." Write one or more words on each line.

The two basic types of memory are   short-term memory   and

(1)

_____. Information stays in short-term memory for

(2)

_____. Then, if it is not important, the information

(3)

_____. When information is important to

(4)

remember, it has to enter _____. That is where new

(5)

_____ are formed among brain cells. You make them

(6)

stronger each time you _____ the information.

(7)

Discussion

Talk about these questions in a small group.

1. What is a "tip of the tongue" experience? Have you ever had one?

2. What advice does the reading give students?

3. What helps you remember new words in English?

4. How do you study vocabulary for a test?

5. What kinds of words are easy to remember? What kinds of words are hard?

Using New Words

Work with a partner. Choose five target words or phrases from the chart on page 155. On a piece of paper, use each word or phrase in a sentence.

Writing

Choose Discussion question 3, 4, or 5 and write a paragraph about it. If you wish, you can begin:

- Several things help me remember new words in English.
- I have several ways to study vocabulary for a test.
- Certain kinds of new words are easier to remember than others.

CHAPTER 15

Sleep and the Brain

Napping

GETTING READY TO READ

Talk with a partner or in a small group.

1. How many hours of sleep do you usually get?

2. Would you like to sleep more? Less? Explain why.

3. Do you think these statements are true or false?

   a. Our brains are completely at rest (they "turn off") when we sleep.　　　　　　　　　　T　　F

   b. We spend only 2–4 percent of a night's sleep time dreaming.　　　　　　　　　　　　T　　F

   c. Sleeping during the day can be good for your brain.　　　　　　　　　　　　　　　T　　F

Look for the answers to question 3, items a–c, in the reading.

READING

Look at the picture, words, and definitions next to the reading. Then read without stopping.

Sleep and the Brain

1   Human beings, like all mammals,[1] need sleep. Adults need an average of 7.5 hours a night. However, the average amount of sleep might not be right for you, just as the average-size shoe might not be right for your foot. The usual sleep **schedule**—doing all your sleeping at night—might not be right for you, either. Getting some sleep during the day may be just what your brain needs.

2   We may not all need the same amount of sleep or the same sleep schedule, but everyone needs the same two types of sleep. Our sleep is **divided** between REM sleep and NREM sleep (which you can **pronounce** "en-rem" or "non-rem"):

- *REM* comes from the words "rapid[2] eye movement." During this type of sleep, your eyes move quickly. This eye movement shows that your brain is very **active** and you are dreaming. You spend about 20 percent of the night in REM sleep.

- *NREM* means "non-REM," or no eye movement. This is dreamless sleep, and it has four stages.

3   When you fall asleep, you enter Stage 1 of NREM sleep. This is a light sleep, so a noise could easily wake you up. After several minutes, you enter Stage 2. It is not so easy to wake you from this type of sleep. Stages 3 and 4 are **periods** of deep sleep. You breathe slowly, your muscles[3] relax, your heart **rate** slows, and your brain becomes less active.

4   You experience both REM and NREM sleep when you go through a sleep cycle. A cycle is a group of events that happen again and again, like the cycle of seasons that happens each year. A sleep cycle takes you from light sleep to deep sleep and back again. It **includes** the four stages of NREM sleep, then a short period of REM sleep, and finally a return to light, NREM sleep. At night, most people go through a **series** of four to six sleep cycles.

(continued)

[1] *mammals* = animals that get milk from their mothers when young

[2] *rapid* = fast

[3] *muscles*

5   It is good to understand sleep cycles and the stages of NREM sleep if you ever take **naps** during the day. A nap of 20 to 45 minutes will mean getting mostly Stage 2 sleep. It will mean sharper motor skills[4] and a better ability to **focus** your mind. That is exactly what most people hope for when they take a nap.

6   A longer nap may not do you as much good.[5] It may mean that you enter the deep sleep of Stage 3 or 4. If your alarm clock rings during deep sleep, you will wake up unable to think clearly. You will probably feel **worse** than you did before your nap, and it can take 30 minutes or more to **get over** this feeling.

7   However, a longer nap can do you good if it covers a full sleep cycle. That takes 90 to 120 minutes. If your alarm wakes you up at the end of a full sleep cycle, you will be coming out of a light sleep, and your brain will have all the advantages[6] of a good rest. Those good **effects** can last for **up to** 10 hours.

8   If you live a busy life, you probably do not always get a full night's sleep. Not getting enough sleep can mean you forget words, you have trouble learning, and you react[7] more slowly. You can probably think of other effects of too little sleep. So consider taking a nap, for the good of your brain, and think about sleep stages if you **set** an alarm.

[4] *motor skills* = skills that depend on the body's nerves and muscles

[5] *do you good* = make you feel better

[6] *advantages* = things that help you do better and be more successful

[7] *react* = feel or do something because of something that just happened

Quick Comprehension Check

 A **Read these sentences. Circle T (true) or F (false).**

1. All adults need the same amount of sleep each night.   T   F

2. We experience two basic types of sleep.   T   F

3. Your eyes move when you dream.   T   F

4. During REM sleep, you dream.   T   F

5. During REM sleep, you go through several stages.   T   F

6. Sleep stages affect how you feel after a nap.   T   F

B Look back at the True/False statements on page 162. Do you want to change any of your answers?

EXPLORING VOCABULARY

Thinking about the Target Vocabulary

 Find the six nouns and two adjectives in **bold** in "Sleep and the Brain." Add them to the chart. Use the singular form of any plural noun.

	Nouns	Verbs	Adjectives	Other
1				
2		divide		
		pronounce		
3				
4		include		
5				
		focus		
6				
		get over		
7				
				up to
8		set		

B Which words are new to you? Circle them in the chart. Then find the words in the reading. Look at the context. Can you guess the meaning?

Using the Target Vocabulary

 A These sentences are **about the reading**. Complete them with the words and phrases in the box.

active	effects	get over	rate	set
divided	focus	includes	series	up to

1. Our sleep is _____ between two types of sleep. We spend part of the night in REM sleep and part in NREM sleep.

2. During REM sleep, when you are dreaming, your brain is _____. It is not at rest.

3. Your heart _____ tells how fast your heart is working. For example, it may beat 60 or 70 times a minute.

4. REM sleep and NREM sleep are both part of a sleep cycle. A sleep cycle _____ both types of sleep.

5. During the night, you go through a _____ of four to six sleep cycles. The cycles happen one after another, in order: the first cycle, then the second, the third, and so on.

6. When you need to pay attention to one thing and one thing only, you have to _____ your mind.

7. Sometimes you wake up from a nap feeling terrible, and you can't think clearly. It takes time to _____ this feeling. (This verb also refers to getting back to good health from being sick or hurt.)

8. Forgetting words, thinking more slowly, getting angry more easily— these are some of the _____, or results, of not getting enough sleep.

9. The effects of a good nap can last _____ ten hours. Ten hours is the greatest amount of time.

10. When you _____ your alarm clock, you move some part of it so that it is ready to ring at the time you want.

B   These sentences use the target words and phrases **in new contexts.** Complete them with the words and phrases in the box.

active	effect	get over	rates	set
divided	focus	included	series	up to

1. One hundred _____ by two is fifty.
2. Some animals sleep during the day and are _____ at night.
3. I turned on the oven and _____ the temperature to 350 degrees.
4. *Superman—The Movie* was the first in a long _____ of Superman movies.
5. The car can hold _____ five people.
6. It takes me a week to ten days to_____ a cold.
7. There was a lot of noise outside the classroom, making it hard for the students to _____.
8. All her English practice had a great _____ on her skills.
9. Children learn at different _____. Some learn quickly, others more slowly.
10. My class _____ students from South America. Two of my classmates were Colombian.

C   Read these sentences. Write the **boldfaced** words next to their definitions on page 168.

a. How do you **pronounce** your last name?
b. Each **period** at the high school is fifty minutes long.
c. Dad sometimes takes a **nap** in the big chair in front of the TV.
d. The boss has a very full **schedule** this week.
e. If I feel **worse** tomorrow, I'll call the doctor.

Target Words	Definitions
1. _____	= not as good (the opposite of *better*)
2. _____	= an amount of time
3. _____	= a short period of sleep during the day
4. _____	= say the sound of a letter or word the correct way
5. _____	= a plan of what someone is going to do, or what is going to happen, and when

Building on the Vocabulary: Word Grammar

The verb *affect* and the noun *effect* are different.
- Use *affect* to mean "make changes in": *Will missing class affect my grade?*
- Use *effect* to refer to a result: *All that candy had a bad effect on her teeth.*

A **Complete the sentences with *affects* or *effects*.**

1. The weather often _____ my plans for the weekend.
2. I'm feeling the _____ of too little sleep.
3. A cold usually _____ your ability to smell things.
4. The new drug is not yet for sale. Researchers are still studying its

   _____.

B **Write your own sentences with *affect* and *effect*.**

1. _____

2. _____

DEVELOPING YOUR SKILLS

Reading for Details

Are these statements about the reading true of false? If the reading doesn't give the information, check (✓) *It doesn't say.*

	True	False	It doesn't say.
1. The average person needs 7.5 hours of sleep a night.	☐	☐	☐
2. The two basic types of sleep are REM and NREM sleep.	☐	☐	☐
3. People's eyes move quickly during NREM sleep.	☐	☐	☐
4. Most people never remember any dreams.	☐	☐	☐
5. Stage 1 sleep is very light.	☐	☐	☐
6. People spend about half the night in Stage 2 sleep.	☐	☐	☐
7. People start dreaming during Stage 3 sleep.	☐	☐	☐
8. A nap of 20 to 45 minutes usually helps the brain work better.	☐	☐	☐
9. A longer nap always makes you feel better than a short nap.	☐	☐	☐
10. Sleeping too many hours a day has bad effects on people.	☐	☐	☐

Cause and Effect

Use information from the reading to complete the diagram of causes and effects.

Cause		Effect
1. brain activity while you sleep	→	dreaming and rapid eye movement
2. a nap of 20–45 minutes	→	
3.	→	feeling tired and unable to think clearly
4. a nap that lasts a full sleep cycle	→	
5.	→	forgetting words, trouble learning, slower reactions

Summarizing

Complete this summary of "Sleep and the Brain." Write one or more words on each line.

People need different amounts of _____, but everyone
                                                    (1)

needs the same _____: REM and NREM sleep. We dream during
                            (2)

_____ and our _____ move quickly. During NREM
           (3)   (4)

sleep, we go through four _____, from light sleep to deep sleep.
                                          (5)

Understanding sleep can help you plan a good _____. A nap
                                                              (6)

can _____, or it can make you feel worse.
              (7)

Interview

How sleepy are you? Work with a partner, and take turns asking the questions below.* Write your partner's answers. Use numbers:

0 = No   1 = Probably not   2 = Maybe   3 = Probably

Would you fall asleep while you were . . .	
1. sitting and reading?	
2. watching TV?	
3. riding in a car for an hour?	
4. lying down in the afternoon?	
5. sitting and talking to someone?	
6. sitting quietly after lunch?	
7. sitting in a car that is stopped in traffic for a few minutes?	
Your partner's total:	

Add up the numbers, and tell your partner the total.

0–6: That's great! You're getting enough sleep.

7–8: You're average.

9 and up: Get more sleep!

*Based on the Epworth Sleepiness Scale designed by Murray W. Johns, M.D.

Using New Words

Work with a partner. Choose five target words or phrases from the chart on page 165. On a piece of paper, use each word or phrase in a sentence.

Writing

Are you a light sleeper (everything wakes you up) or a heavy sleeper (nothing wakes you up)? Do you get enough sleep in general? What happens when you don't get enough? Write a paragraph about yourself as a sleeper.

CHAPTER 16

In Your Dreams

The idea for the story of Frankenstein came to writer Mary Shelley in a dream.

GETTING READY TO READ

Talk in a small group or with the whole class.

1. What do you learn from the pictures and caption above?
2. How often do you remember your dreams?
3. What do you remember about your dreams?
4. Do you think people can get good ideas while they're sleeping?
5. Do you think people can find the answers to problems while they sleep?
6. Do you think animals dream?

READING

Look at the pictures, words, and definitions next to the reading. Then read without stopping.

In Your Dreams

1   Bruno Beckham has a good job. He also has a new job offer. He has to make a decision **right away**, but he is not sure **whether** he should accept the offer. He is sure, however, that he is not going to make up his mind tonight. "I'll know in the morning," he says. How will he know? What does he think will happen overnight?[1] "I don't know," he says, "but **whenever** I have a big decision to make, I have to sleep on it."

2   When you face a big decision, do your friends tell you to sleep on it? People in Italy say, "Dormici su." It means the same thing. In France, they say, "La nuit porte conseil," meaning "The night brings advice." People in many cultures believe that something **useful** happens during sleep, but what happens, and why?

3   Maybe the answer can be found in our dreams. Many people believe that dreams help us in our **daily** lives. The famous German composer[2] Beethoven believed this. He said that he wrote music that came to him in dreams. The American boxer[3] Floyd Patterson believed it, too. He used to dream of new ways to move in a fight, and he **claimed** that these moves helped him surprise other boxers. Srinivasa Ramanujan, an important mathematician[4] from India, said that all his **discoveries** came to him in dreams. Artists, scientists, and writers report getting ideas from dreams, too. The English writer Mary Shelley did. She said that the story of Frankenstein came to her in a dream.

4   Scientists do not agree on what dreams mean or why people dream. Some say that dreams have no meaning and no **purpose**. They say that dreams show **activity** in the brain, but it is like the activity of a car going in circles with no driver. It does nothing useful. **On the other hand**, some scientists claim that dreams are helpful. They say that dreams are good for learning new skills and developing strong memories.

[1] *overnight* = continuing all night

[2] a *composer* = a writer of music

[3] a *boxer*

[4] a *mathematician* = someone who does research in math

(continued)

5   Some researchers hope to learn more about the dreams of people by studying the dreams of animals. At the Massachusetts Institute of Technology (MIT), scientists have studied the dreams of rats. During the day, the rats were learning to run through a maze,[5] and the scientists were **recording** the activity in the rats' brains. Later, during REM sleep, the rats' brains showed exactly the same activity. The rats were going through the maze again in their dreams. Researchers could tell if the dreaming rats were running or standing **still**. In fact, MIT researcher Matthew Wilson reported, "We can pinpoint[6] where they would be in the maze if they were awake."

[5] a rat in a *maze*

[6] *pinpoint* = show exactly where something is without any mistake

6   Were the rats practicing for the next day? Does dreaming **somehow** help them learn and remember? Do human brains work this way? Wilson and his team **are searching** for the answers to these questions. Right now, there is no **explanation** for dreams that everyone accepts. There is a great deal we do not know about the sleeping brain, but maybe one day we will know all its secrets.

Matthew Wilson's words come from an article by Sarah Smith, "Caught in a Maze," *Psychology Today* 34, no. 3 (May 2001): 20.

Quick Comprehension Check

Read these sentences. Circle T (true) or F (false).

1. Bruno Beckham says sleep helps him make decisions.   T   F

2. Many people think dreams help us.   T   F

3. According to some famous people, good ideas come in dreams.   T   F

4. Scientists all agree: There is one basic reason why we dream.   T   F

5. Scientists say dreams are bad for your brain.   T   F

6. Only human beings dream.   T   F

EXPLORING VOCABULARY

Thinking about the Target Vocabulary

 A Find the four nouns, three verbs, and two adjectives in **bold** in "In Your Dreams." Add them to the chart. Use the singular form of any plural noun and the base form of each verb.

	Nouns	Verbs	Adjectives	Other
1				right away
				whether
				whenever
2				
3				
4				
				on the other hand
5				
				still
6				somehow

 B Which words are new to you? Circle them in the chart. Then find the words in the reading. Look at the context. Can you guess the meaning?

Using the Target Vocabulary

 A These sentences are **about the reading**. Complete them with the words and phrases in the box.

activity	explanation	still	whether
are searching	on the other hand	useful	
claimed	somehow	whenever	

1. Bruno doesn't know _____ to accept his new job offer. He doesn't know if he wants to accept it.

2. Every time that he faces a big decision, Bruno sleeps on it. This means, _____ Bruno has a big decision to make, he waits until morning.

3. Many people believe something _____ happens while we sleep, something that helps us.

4. The boxer Floyd Patterson _____ that his dreams helped him win fights. Was it true? No one knows for sure. However, that is what he said.

5. Dreams show _____ in the brain. Something is happening there.

6. Some scientists say that dreams have no effect on us. _____, others say that dreams help us learn and remember.

7. Sometimes the rats moved through the maze. At other times, they stood _____ (not moving).

8. Did dreaming help the rats in some way? Did it _____ help them remember where to go in the maze?

9. The researchers at MIT _____ for answers to the question "Why do we dream?" They are trying to find answers.

10. So far, no one has explained dreams in a way that everyone accepts. We have no good _____ for them.

**These sentences use the target words and phrases in new contexts.
Complete them with the words and phrases in the box.**

activity	explanation	still	whether
are searching	on the other hand	useful	
claimed	somehow	whenever	

1. The police _____ for the missing child.

2. You must sit _____ when I take your picture.

3. Gloria couldn't decide _____ to cut her hair.

4. In general, the stores are busier _____ it rains.

5. I don't know how he did it, but _____, he managed to win.

6. Fred is so busy that he never seems to sit down! His days are full of _____.

7. I don't understand why Helen was so upset. Did she give you any _____?

8. You want to store _____ facts in long-term memory so that you'll remember them later.

9. Bob _____ that his dog could read his mind, but I think Bob was imagining things.

10. Chris has two job offers. The first one pays better; _____, the second one sounds more secure. A secure job versus* a better-paying one—which is more important?

* The Latin word *versus* is often abbreviated as *vs.* or *v.* It means "as opposed to or against" and is used for two things being compared, two sports teams going against each other, or the two sides in a court case.

Read each definition and look at the paragraph number. Look back at the reading on pages 173–174 to find the boldfaced word or phrase to match the definition. Copy it in the chart.

Definition	Paragraph	Target Word or Phrase
1. very soon, immediately	1	
2. happening every day	3	
3. new facts, or answers to a question, that someone learns	3	
4. a reason for doing something	4	
5. storing sounds or pictures on something so they can be listened to or seen again	5	

Building on the Vocabulary: Studying Collocations

Several phrases with *right* + adverb mean "immediately" or "very soon." Look at these examples of phrases with *right*:

- *I need the money **right away**.*
- *I'm coming **right back**. / I'll be **right back**.*
- *We're leaving **right now**.*

Write three sentences using the three phrases above with *right*.

1. _____

2. _____

3. _____

DEVELOPING YOUR SKILLS

Fact vs. Opinion

> Use *fact* to refer to a piece of information that can be shown to be true. Use *opinion* to refer to what someone believes but cannot show is true.

 A **Decide if each statement is a fact or an opinion. Base your answers on information from the reading. Circle** *Fact* **or** *Opinion***.**

1. There is activity in the brain while we sleep.   (Fact)/ Opinion

2. Our dreams are useful.   Fact / Opinion

3. Some famous people have believed in the power of dreams.   Fact / Opinion

4. Dreams help us learn new skills.   Fact / Opinion

5. MIT scientists have studied the dreams of rats.   Fact / Opinion

6. In the future, scientists will discover why we dream.   Fact / Opinion

B **Write two sentences.**

1. Write a fact about dreams from "In Your Dreams."

   _____

   _____

2. Write an opinion of your own about dreams.

   _____

   _____

Summarizing

Write answers to these seven questions on a piece of paper. Then use your answers to write a summary of the reading. Write your summary as a paragraph.

1. When do people say "sleep on it"?
2. Why do they say it?

3. What do some people say dreams can do?

4. What example can you give of dreams being useful to someone?

5. What do scientists say about the meaning and purpose of dreams?

6. Why do scientists study the dreams of animals?

7. What is one possible reason for dreaming?

   If you wish, you can begin:

   People often say, "Sleep on it!" to someone who needs to make a big decision. They think something helpful happens in our brains while we sleep and dream. . . .

Sharing Opinions

Talk about these questions in a small group.

1. Is it important to remember and think about your dreams? Why or why not?

2. Would you like someone to tell you the meaning of your dreams? Why or why not?

3. Do you believe people can learn while they sleep? Why or why not?

Using New Words

Work with a partner. Choose five target words or phrases from the chart on page 175. On a piece of paper, use each word or phrase in a sentence.

Writing

Choose a topic. Write a paragraph.

1. Whenever Bruno Beckham faces a big decision, he sleeps on it. What do you do? What, or who, helps you make decisions? How?

2. Think about a time when you had to make a choice. What did you decide? How did you make your decision? Do you think it was the right one? Why or why not?

Wrap-up

REVIEWING VOCABULARY

 Complete the sentences with words and phrases from the box. There are two extra words or phrases.

according to	on the other hand	search	that is
get over	or so	somehow	whenever
no matter	right away	supplies	whether

1. I don't know _____ I'll go or stay. I have to make up my mind.

2. He says he has to have it, _____ what the price is!

3. _____ the weather report, the rain should end soon.

4. Come _____ you want. I'll be home all day.

5. The lecturer spoke for an hour _____.

6. Call if you need me, and I'll come _____.

7. His hourly rate is awfully high; _____, he does excellent work.

8. He didn't have a ticket, but he _____ managed to talk his way in to see the show.

9. The farm _____ several local restaurants with fresh vegetables.

10. You can _____ the Internet for the information you need.

Complete the sentences with words from the box. There are two extra words.

affect	concerns	include	periods	realize	series
claims	discovery	meant	purpose	review	term

1. He had a lot of homework. That _____ that he couldn't go out.

2. Her research _____ the connections between sleep and memory.

3. Why do we have to do this? What's the _____?

4. Does the rent for the apartment _____ heat and electricity, or is that extra?

5. Reporters had many questions about the scientist's latest

   _____.

6. After a long _____ of meetings, they came to an agreement.

7. One driver _____ that the other driver was going too fast.

8. How will the new law _____ the average taxpayer?

9. We expect a cloudy weekend with some _____ of rain.

10. Unfortunately, he didn't _____ how long it would take to get there.

EXPANDING VOCABULARY

Choose the correct member from each word family to complete sentences 1–8 below.

	Nouns	Verbs	Adjectives	Adverbs
1.	activity		active	actively
2.	creation	create	creative	creatively
3.	effect		effective	effectively
4.	emotion		emotional	emotionally
5.	increase	increase	increasing	increasingly
6.	luck		lucky	luckily
7.	use	use	useful	usefully
8.	weakness	weaken	weak	weakly

1. The brain is _____ during REM sleep.
2. The government reported the _____ of 50,000 new jobs.
3. His family troubles are having an _____ on his work.
4. She studies how children develop _____.
5. _____ numbers of people are questioning the president's decision.
6. _____, she managed to get to the station in time for her train.
7. He bought a new computer and now has no _____ for his old one.
8. Powerful storms over the ocean usually _____ as they pass over land.

PLAYING WITH WORDS

There are 12 target words from Unit 4 in this puzzle. The words go across (→) and down (↓). Find the words and circle them. Then use them to complete the sentences below.

X	I	Q	V	X	A	N	Y	M	O	R	E
K	M	H	M	R	E	G	I	O	N	V	X
L	M	W	P	D	X	P	W	Q	V	X	P
F	E	E	D	G	Z	R	S	T	I	L	L
W	D	Z	K	W	J	O	X	W	W	H	A
Z	I	J	V	X	P	N	V	O	Z	K	N
D	A	I	L	Y	K	O	X	R	J	X	A
X	T	V	X	G	Q	U	P	S	E	T	T
W	E	I	G	H	T	N	Z	E	K	W	I
T	L	X	Z	K	W	C	J	X	W	Z	O
H	Y	C	O	N	N	E	C	T	I	O	N

Across

1. Do they see the _____ between human activity and changes in the weather?
2. We _____ our cat twice a day.
3. Please stand _____ while I take your picture.
4. He's trying to lose _____ by eating less and walking more.
5. His _____ schedule is very full.
6. That _____ of France is famous for cheese.
7. Naturally, they're _____ about the tax increase.
8. She used to wear leather, but she doesn't _____.

Down

1. The boss will expect an _____ when you're late for work.
2. How do you _____ your last name?
3. They called 911 and the police came __immediately__.
4. He's not getting over his cold—it's getting _____.

BUILDING DICTIONARY SKILLS

Many words have more than one meaning. When you look up a word in the dictionary, you may need to read through several meanings to find the one you need.

A Look at this entry for the verb *set*. Write the number of the meaning used in each sentence below.

__2__ 1. His parents want him to **set** an example for his little brother.

____ 2. **Set** the timer for five minutes.

____ 3. Have they **set** a date for their wedding?

____ 4. Please **set** the boxes on that table.

B Look at this entry for the verb *apply*. Write the number of the meaning used in each sentence below.

____ 1. The new rule **applies** to all students.

____ 2. We **applied** two coats of paint.

____ 3. He is **applying** to six

set¹ /sɛt/ *v* past tense and past participle **set**, present participle **setting**
1 ‣ PUT STH SOMEWHERE ‣ [T] to carefully put something down somewhere: *Just set that bag **down** on the floor.* | *He took off his watch and **set** it **on** the dresser.*
2 ‣ STANDARD ‣ [T] to decide something that other things are compared to or measured against: *The agency has **set** standards for water cleanliness.* | *Parents should **set** an example for their children* (=behave in the way they want their children to behave).
3 ‣ PRICE/TIME ETC. ‣ [T] to decide that something will happen at a particular time, cost a particular amount, etc.: *The judge plans to **set** a **date** for the trial.* | *Officials have not yet **set** a **price** on how much the study will cost.*
4 ‣ CLOCK/MACHINE ‣ [T] to move part of a clock or a piece of equipment so that it will do what you want it to do: *I **set** my **alarm** for 6:30.* | *Do you know how to set the VCR?*
5 ‣ START STH HAPPENING ‣ [I,T] to make something start happening or to make someone start doing something: *Angry mobs **set** the building **on fire**.* |

ap•ply /əˈplaɪ/ *v* (**applied**, **applies**)   **1** [I] to make a formal, especially written, request for a job, place at a college, permission to do something, etc.: *Fifteen people **applied for** the job.* | *He has **applied for** U.S. citizenship.* | *Anna **applied to** several colleges in California.*   **2** [I,T] to have an effect on, involve or concern a particular person, group, or situation: *The nutrition labeling requirements **apply to** most foods.*   **3** [T] to use a method, idea, etc. in a particular situation, activity, or process: *Internships give students a chance to apply their skills in real situations.*   **4** [T] to put something on a surface or press on the surface of something: *Apply the lotion evenly.*

colleges.

Circle the letter of the word or phrase that best completes each sentence.

Example:

Thousands of people were in the streets to _____ in the celebration.

  a. explain   **b.** pick up   **c.** take part   **d.** discover

1. They never keep large _____ of money in the store.

  a. scores   **b.** amounts   **c.** movements   **d.** weights

2. Neighbors offered to help Tina _____ for her lost cat.

  a. pronounce   **b.** support   **c.** search   **d.** include

3. I don't know _____ how much it costs, but it's expensive.

  a. exactly   **b.** immediately   **c.** whenever   **d.** toward

4. He believes in "Murphy's law." _____, he believes that if anything can go wrong, it will.

  a. Luckily   **b.** Or so   **c.** All of a sudden **d.** That is

5. The fire _____ the building, but no one was hurt.

  a. destroyed   **b.** created   **c.** caused   **d.** developed

6. He needs more time to _____ his mind.

  a. make sure   **b.** pay attention **c.** work out   **d.** make up

7. A video game _____ is responsible for a team of people who develop games.

  a. software   **b.** producer   **c.** professor   **d.** period

8. People from TV and radio were there to _____ the president's every word.

a. divide   **b.** suggest   **c.** record   **d.** feed

9. _____, they can't afford to go back to visit their old friends very often.

  a. Outdoors   **b.** Right away   **c.** Anymore   **d.** Unfortunately

10. When a problem like this _____, it's best to deal with it quickly.

  a. comes up   **b.** gives up   **c.** gets over   **d.** ends up

11. He writes _____ for a computer software company.

  a. purposes   **b.** labs   **c.** subjects   **d.** programs

12. Not everyone will be invited, only _____ people.

  a. upset   **b.** certain   **c.** daily   **d.** entire

13. We waited thirty minutes at the restaurant until there was a table _____.

  a. relaxed   **b.** active   **c.** available   **d.** useful

14. Her father made her turn off the TV and _____ on her homework.

  a. focus   **b.** sound   **c.** apply   **d.** claim

15. Your heart _____ goes up when you run.

  a. case   **b.** stage   **c.** rate   **d.** increase

16. Nothing seems to help, _____ what I try.

  a. no matter   **b.** on the other hand   **c.** as a matter of fact   **d.** first of all

17. He said he was a salesman and asked me, "What do you _____?"

  a. set   **b.** concern   **c.** refer   **d.** do

18. It was terrible news, and we found it difficult to control our _____.

  a. seasons   **b.** emotions   **c.** hardware   **d.** discoveries

19. Please stay _____ but get out of the building as fast as you can.

    a. worse   **b.** calm   **c.** weak   **d.** advanced

20. The area known as the Farm Belt _____ most of the nation's meat and grains.

    a. supplies   **b.** gets into   **c.** reviews   **d.** realizes

21. He speaks and writes well. His _____ skills are strong.

    a. secure   **b.** training   **c.** communication **d.** activity

22. She wants to study art, but her parents want her to go into _____.

    a. field   **b.** region   **c.** connection   **d.** medicine

23. The doctor's quiet voice and _____ touch made his young patients trust him.

    a. international **b.** medical   **c.** gentle   **d.** sharp

24. A kind of _____ that is new to the area is hurting several kinds of trees.

    a. needle   **b.** insect   **c.** forest   **d.** leather

25. Is there room to store these things in your _____?

    a. patience   **b.** interview   **c.** closet   **d.** nap

26. They are showing a _____ of films, starting at 4:00 P.M. and ending after midnight.

    a. series   **b.** explanation **c.** tool   **d.** effect

27. All this snow will no doubt _____ more road accidents.

    a. contain   **b.** mean   **c.** manage to   **d.** schedule

28. _____ the newspapers, no one was seriously hurt.

    a. Somehow   **b.** According to **c.** By accident **d.** Still

29. The plane can hold _____ 120 people.

    a. affect   **b.** apply   **c.** whether   **d.** up to

30. After class, the students reviewed their _____ to prepare for the test.

    a. lecture   **b.** term   **c.** notes   **d.** influence

See the Answer Key on page 239.

UNIT
5

COMMUNICATION

Who Does It Better?

*African elephants—in
conversation?*

GETTING READY TO READ

Talk with a partner or in a small group.

Do human beings and animals communicate in each of the ways listed
below? Circle Yes or No. For each *yes* answer, give an example.

	Words	Sounds	Movements	Smells
Humans	(Yes)　Hello	Yes	Yes	Yes
	No	No	No	No
Animals	Yes	Yes	Yes	Yes
	No	No	No	No

Share your answers with the rest of the class.

READING

Look at the pictures, words, and definitions next to the reading. Then read without stopping. Don't worry about new words. Don't stop to use a dictionary. Just keep reading!

Who Does It Better?

1   Who is better at communicating, people or animals? If you think about human inventions such as the telephone and the Internet, the answer to this question seems perfectly clear. Human beings are "The Great Communicators." However, think about your own **personal** communication skills. If you compare what you can do with what certain animals can do, then the answer is not so simple. Animals can do things that people cannot.

2   Most of us depend on our **voices** for much of our communication. We use words and sounds to pass information to the people around us. However, the sound of the human voice cannot travel very far. Even the voice of an opera singer[1] with years of training cannot be heard as well as many animal voices. Think of the elephant, for example. Its voice is very **powerful** because of the elephant's great size, so it can be heard for miles. Elephants can make very **low** sounds, too, sounds too deep for any human to hear, which let them communicate over even longer **distances**. These sounds travel in sound **waves** through the air and through **the ground**. How do elephants receive messages like these? No one knows. Maybe they hear them with their ears, or maybe they **sense** them in some other way. It is possible that the sound waves pass from the ground through the elephants' toenails[2] into their bones and then to their brains!

3   Let's also consider communication **through** movement. For example, some people use dance to share ideas or emotions, and when we watch these dancers, we may understand what they are thinking or feeling. But even a great dancer's ability to speak through movement cannot match the average honeybee's.[3] Bees do a very special dance to tell other bees where to find food. The dance tells the other bees which way to go so that they can fly in a **straight** line to the food. It also tells them exactly how far to

[1] an *opera singer*

[2] an elephant's *toenails*

[3] a *honeybee*

(continued)

go. It gives clear information about both the **direction** and the distance to a specific place.

4   Many animals communicate through smells. A smell can carry a lot of information. For example, a smell can say, "This is my place—get out!" or a smell can give an invitation. Often a **female** animal who wants a **male** animal to come to her will produce a smell to **attract** him. It tells him, "Here I am—come and find me." Human beings also receive messages through their noses, as when someone's nose receives the message, "There is something good cooking in the kitchen." But people do not usually use smells to communicate, and our noses do not receive messages very well. We certainly cannot **compete** with the great white shark.[4] A large part of its brain—14 percent of it—is just for interpreting[5] smells in the ocean.

[4] a *great white shark*

[5] *interpreting* = figuring out the meaning of

5   Our noses are not the best, our voices are not the strongest, and our dancing may not say anything at all. But people are the only ones with words and written languages. So, maybe we can still call ourselves "The Great Communicators."

Quick Comprehension Check

Read these sentences. Circle T (true) or F (false).

1. Humans communicate better than animals in every way.   T   F

2. Elephants can make sounds that travel far.   T   F

3. Bees can communicate with other bees through movement.   T   F

4. A honeybee dances to tell other bees about danger.   T   F

5. Both animals and people use their noses to get information.   T   F

6. The great white shark is good at understanding smells in the ocean.   T   F

EXPLORING VOCABULARY

Thinking about the Target Vocabulary

 A **Find the five nouns, three verbs, and six adjectives in bold in "Who Does It Better?" Add them to the chart. Write them in the order they appear in the reading. Use the singular form of any plural noun and the base form of each verb.**

	Nouns	Verbs	Adjectives	Other
1				
2				
3				through
4				

B **Which words are new to you? Circle them in the chart. Then find the words in the reading. Look at the context. Can you guess the meaning?**

Using the Target Vocabulary

 These sentences are about the reading. Complete them with the words in the box.

attract	direction	male	powerful	through
compete	low	personal	sense	voice

1. Each person has his or her own _____ communication skills. These are the skills that belong to that one person.

2. When you speak or sing, you use your _____. Other people hear it.

3. The voice of an elephant is strong and loud. It has a lot of power. It is _____ enough to be heard far away.

4. Elephants can make sounds that are not high enough for the human ear. These are very _____ sounds. (Other animals, such as dogs, can hear sounds that are too high for us to hear.)

5. Elephants hear with their ears. They may also _____ very low sounds through their toenails. It is not clear how they become aware of these sounds.

6. Some animals, like bees, communicate _____ movement. They use movement.

7. The bee's dance tells other bees the _____ to fly in— which way to go.

8. A female animal may produce a smell to get the attention of a _____ animal. She wants him to know where she is.

9. When a female wants a male to come to her, she tries to _____ him, or make him interested in her.

10. Humans should not try to _____ with the great white shark in the ability to smell. The shark would always win.

These sentences use the target words **in new contexts**. Complete them with the words in the box.

attracted	direction	male	powerful	through
compete	low	personal	sensed	voices

1. Hurricanes and typhoons are _____ storms.

2. The scientist made his discoveries _____ years of hard work.

3. At night, the light _____ insects, so we turned it off.

4. The driver turned the car around and drove away in the opposite _____.

5. My mother didn't say anything, but I _____ that something was wrong.

6. Men usually have lower _____ than women do.

7. He has learned about the business world both in school and through his own _____ experience.

8. Athletes from many countries _____ at the Olympic games.

9. _____ animals are often larger than female animals of the same kind.

10. A piano makes _____ sounds when you play the keys on the left end.

Read these sentences. Match the boldfaced target words and phrases with their definitions.

a. Make sure you plant the tree a safe **distance** from the house.

b. *Waitress* is a word sometimes used for a **female** server in a restaurant.

c. Leaves fell from the trees and covered **the ground**.

d. We placed the chairs in a **straight** line.

e. Light and sound move in **waves**.

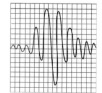

A way to picture
sound waves

Target Words and Phrases	Definitions
1. _____	= the surface of the earth; what you walk on outdoors
2. _____	= going in one direction only, not bending or curving
3. _____	= the amount of space between two places or things
4. _____	= belonging to the sex that can have babies or produce eggs
5. _____	= the form in which some types of energy move

Building on the Vocabulary: Word Grammar

The word *low* is usually an adjective. It can describe
- a quiet or deep sound: *a low whisper, a low voice*
- something that isn't high or tall: *a low wall, a low building*
- a small amount or number: *low-fat food, low grades*
- the bad nature of something: *a low opinion, a low trick*

Low can also be
- an adverb (*The plane was flying low.*)
- a noun (*Prices fell to a new low.*)

A **Is *low* a noun, an adjective, or an adverb in each sentence? Circle your answers.**

1. The TV sits on a low table.	*n.*	*adj.*	*adv.*
2. Everybody's life has its highs and lows.	*n.*	*adj.*	*adv.*
3. Shoppers like low prices.	*n.*	*adj.*	*adv.*
4. He threw the ball low.	*n.*	*adj.*	*adv.*
5. I got a low score on the test.	*n.*	*adj.*	*adv.*

B **Write three sentences using *low* in different ways.**

1. _____

_____

2. _____

_____

3. _____

_____

DEVELOPING YOUR SKILLS

Reading for Details

Are these statements about the reading true or false? If the reading doesn't give the information, check (✓) *It doesn't say.*

	True	False	It doesn't say.
1. We depend on our voices for much of our communication with other people.	☐	☐	☐
2. Elephants have the best hearing of any animals.	☐	☐	☐
3. Sound waves can travel only through the air.	☐	☐	☐
4. The dance of the honeybee tells other bees which way to go to find food.	☐	☐	☐
5. The dance of the honeybee tells other bees what kind of food they will find.	☐	☐	☐
6. All living things use smells to communicate.	☐	☐	☐
7. Most of a great white shark's brain is used for reading smells in the ocean.	☐	☐	☐
8. Words give human beings a very special way to communicate.	☐	☐	☐

Understanding Topics of Paragraphs

Complete this diagram of the reading. Write the topics of paragraphs 2, 3, and 4. You do not need to write complete sentences.

Who Does It Better?

1 (Introduction) *People vs. animals—comparing communication skills*

2
3
4

5 (Conclusion) *People win—we have words, written language*

Understanding Main Ideas and Supporting Details

 Match the main ideas and the details that support them. Write the letters.

Main Ideas	Supporting Details
_c_ 1. Certain inventions help people communicate.	a. Bees do a dance to tell other bees where food is.
____ 2. The human voice can't travel as far as some animal voices.	b. A female animal may produce a smell to attract a male.
____ 3. Some animals communicate through movement.	c. Think of the telephone and the Internet.
____ 4. Animals sometimes use smells to communicate with other animals.	d. The great white shark has a much better sense of smell than we do.
____ 5. People can't compete with animals in some ways.	e. An elephant's voice can be heard for miles.

Think of another example to support each main idea in Part A. Write complete sentences.

1.   _Inventions like pens and paper let people write to each other._

2.   _____

3.   _____

4.   _____

5.   _____

Discussion

Talk about these questions in a small group.

1. What are four types of communication mentioned in the reading? Give an example of each one.

2. According to the reading, people don't usually communicate through smell. But what are people saying when they put on something such as perfume, cologne, or aftershave?

3. In what ways do people and animals communicate with each other? Think of at least three examples.

Using New Words

Work with a partner. Choose five target words or phrases from the chart on page 193. On a piece of paper, use each word or phrase in a sentence.

Writing

Choose a topic. Write a paragraph.

1. Pets sometimes play an important part in people's lives. People communicate with their pets in several ways. Have you ever had a pet? How do or did you communicate?

2. What kind of animal would you like to be? Why? Tell both the good and the bad things about being this kind of animal.

3. Imagine that you are an animal. Describe a day in your life.

CHAPTER 18

When and Why We Laugh

"The oil in the social machine"

GETTING READY TO READ

Talk in a small group or with the whole class.

1. Look at the picture. What is happening? Name two or more ways these people are communicating.

2. Ask one person in your group to make himself or herself laugh. Then talk about what happened in your group when this person laughed, or tried to.

3. How many people in your group are ticklish?[1]

   [1] *ticklish* = easily made to laugh when someone touches certain parts of your body

READING

Look at the picture, words, and definitions next to the reading. Then read without stopping.

When and Why We Laugh

1   People have many ways to **express** themselves—to show how they feel or what they think. One way that feels especially good is **laughter**. We laugh when we see or hear something funny, and sometimes we laugh just because we see other people laughing. Many people laugh when someone tickles[1] them. Laughter **clearly** has a **role** to play in human communication, but what are we saying when we laugh?

2   A team of psychologists[2] studied the laughter of 120 students at a U.S. university by having the students watch funny movies. Sometimes the students were alone, and sometimes they were in pairs. The psychologists recorded the students' laughter, and they noticed that the students made a wide variety of laughing sounds. They also found that there were differences in how each student laughed and in how many times the student laughed. Both these things depended on his or her partner: Was the other person the same sex or the opposite sex? And what was the relationship between the two—was the person a friend or a **stranger**? Here are some of the researchers' findings:[3]

- Men laughed much more during the movies when they were with a friend. It did not matter whether the friend was male or female. Men laughed much less when their partner was a stranger or when they were alone.

- Women laughed most when they were with male friends. With male strangers, women laughed in a higher voice.

- There were three basic types of laughs: high songlike laughs, laughs with the sounds coming mostly through the nose, and low grunting[4] laughs like the sounds a pig makes.

3   The researchers then **carried out** another **study**, in which they asked people to listen to these three types of laughter. To find out which kind people liked best, they asked questions like: Does the person laughing sound friendly? Do you think he or

[1] *tickle* = touch certain parts of someone's body to make him or her laugh

[2] a *psychologist* = someone trained in the study of the mind and how it works

[3] *findings* = the information that someone learns as a result of research

[4] A pig makes low *grunting* sounds.

she sounds **attractive**? Would you like to meet this person? Most people **preferred** the high songlike sounds and were attracted to people who laughed this way.

4   The researchers believe that laughter is a tool we use, usually without thinking about it, to influence the emotions and **behavior** of other people. We often use laughter to show that we want to be friends. In fact, contrary to[5] what you may think, most laughter during conversation is *not* because someone just heard something funny. Researcher Robert Provine says that in conversation, the people who are listening **actually** laugh less than the ones who are speaking. A speaker's laughter has a **social** purpose, says Provine. He calls laughter "the oil in the social machine." **In other words**, it helps relationships between people work **smoothly**.

[5] *contrary to = completely different from or opposite to*

5   Did you know that humans are not the only ones who laugh? Dogs do, too. Dog laughter sounds something like "Huh, huh, huh," and it seems to express the idea "Let's play!" Another university researcher, Jaak Panksepp, reports that rats laugh, too. They laugh when he tickles them. But please do not go out and try this. Panksepp **warns**, "You have to know the rat."

Robert Provine's words come from "He Who Laughs Less?" *PBS—Scientific American Frontiers: Life's Little Questions II*. Retrieved March 9, 2009, from http://www.pbs.org/saf/1105/features/laughter.htm. Jaak Panksepp was quoted in "Don't Look Now, But Is That Dog Laughing?" *Science News* 160, no. 4 (July 28, 2001): 55.

Quick Comprehension Check

Read these sentences. Circle T (true) or F (false).

1. Laughter is part of human communication.   T   F

2. Researchers have studied why and how people laugh.   T   F

3. The people who are with us affect how we laugh.   T   F

4. The college students in the study laughed only with their friends.   T   F

5. Researchers say that we laugh to influence other people.   T   F

6. Only human beings laugh.   T   F

EXPLORING VOCABULARY

Thinking about the Target Vocabulary

 A Find the five nouns, four verbs, and two adjectives in **bold** in "When and Why We Laugh." Add them to the chart. Use the singular form of any plural noun and the base form of each verb.

	Nouns	Verbs	Adjectives	Other
1				
				clearly
2				
3				
4				
				actually
				in other words
				smoothly
5				

B Which words are new to you? Circle them in the chart. Then find the words in the reading. Look at the context. Can you guess the meaning?

Using the Target Vocabulary

 These sentences are about the reading. Complete them with the words and phrases in the box.

| actually | clearly | in other words | preferred | social |
| behavior | express | laughter | role | warned |

1. People communicate ideas and emotions with words. We can also _____ ourselves with sounds.

2. The sound of _____ sometimes makes other people laugh, too.

3. It is easy to see that laughter is important in communication. _____, it is important.

4. Laughter is useful. It does a certain job. It plays a _____ in communication.

5. Researchers asked people to listen to three types of laughter and choose the one they liked best. Most people _____ the same type.

6. Researchers say we use laughter to influence the _____ of other people—that is, to influence what they do and say.

7. Who laughs more in conversation, the speaker or the listener? Most people would guess the listener, but _____, it is the speaker. (This word often introduces new and surprising information.)

8. Laughter has a _____ purpose: to help people live and work well together.

9. You can use the phrase "_____" to mean "Here is another way to say the same thing." Often the second way is easier to understand.

10. One researcher said to be careful about tickling rats. He _____ people to be careful.

These sentences use the target words and phrases **in new contexts**. Complete them with the words and phrases in the box.

actually	clearly	in other words	prefer	social
behavior	expressed	laughter	role	warns

1. The room was full of the sounds of music, conversation, and

   _____.

2. A neighbor called the boy's parents to talk about his bad

   _____.

3. The sign _____ drivers that the road is bad, so they should be careful.

4. The things you do with other people, especially for fun, make up your _____ life.

5. What would you _____ to do, go to a movie or go out to eat?

6. She claimed to be twenty-one, but she was _____ nineteen.

7. He almost never _____ his feelings or talked about anything personal.

8. I don't know what her job is, but she has an important _____ in the company.

9. _____, it's time for the child's nap. She can't keep her eyes open.

10. This street is a dead end. _____, it doesn't connect with another street, so you can't drive through.

Read these sentences. Match the boldfaced target words and phrases with their definitions.

a. The children's mother warned them not to speak to **strangers**.

b. The scientists were interested in the effects of sleep on memory, so they did a **study**.

c. A group of terrorists **carried out** an attack.

d. Joe traveled for twenty hours and changed planes three times, but the trip went **smoothly**.

e. Most magazines have photos of **attractive** people.

Target Words and Phrases	Definitions
1. _____	= nice or pleasing to look at; interesting
2. _____	= happening without problems or difficulties
3. _____	= people you do not know
4. _____	= did something that needed to be organized and planned
5. _____	= a piece of research done to find out more about a subject or problem

Building on the Vocabulary: Studying Collocations

Some verbs are often followed by a certain preposition. When a verb can take more than one preposition, its meaning may change (for example, *apply + for* vs. *apply + to*.)

Here are some examples of verb + preposition combinations:

apply + to/for	*focus + on*
belong + to	*refer + to*
compete + with/for	*search + for*
depend + on	*worry + about*

A **Complete the sentences. Add the preposition that goes with the verb.**

1. These tools belong _____ my neighbor.
2. I depend _____ my friends for advice.
3. The student's question referred _____ the exam.
4. I worried _____ the interview, but it went well.
5. Are you going to apply _____ the job?
6. He thinks the rules don't apply _____ him!
7. I speak slowly when I have to search _____ the right words.
8. The small bookstores can't compete _____ the big ones.
9. Stores compete _____ customers.
10. Music helps me focus _____ my homework.

B **Write five sentences with verb + preposition combinations from the box.**

1. _____
2. _____
3. _____
4. _____
5. _____

DEVELOPING YOUR SKILLS

Finding Clues to Meaning

Writers use a variety of ways to supply the meaning of a word or phrase in a reading.

- Sometimes a writer follows the word or phrase with a comma (,) or a dash (—) and then a definition or explanation. For example, "Mahmoud was born near Tehran, the largest city in Iran" or "This part of the body is small—only 2–3 percent of your total body weight . . ."

- Sometimes a phrase like *that is* or *in other words* introduces a definition or explanation. For example, "Does the information affect our emotions? That is, does it make us happy, sad, excited, or upset?"

Look at "When and Why We Laugh." Find the definitions or explanations given for the boldfaced phrases below and copy them here.

1. "People have many ways to **express themselves** _____
_____ "

2. "Provine calls laughter '**the oil in the social machine**.' _____
_____ "

Reading for Details

Read these questions about "When and Why We Laugh." Refer back to the reading and write short answers or complete sentences.

1. What are three reasons for laughter?

   a. _____

   b. _____

   c. _____

2. Who did a study on laughter?_____

3. Who was in the study? _____

4. What did the students have to do? _____
_____

5. What did changes in the students' laughter depend on? _____
_____

6. When did the female students in the study laugh most? _____
_____

7. When did the male students laugh most? _____
_____

8. According to researcher Robert Provine, who laughs more during a conversation, the person speaking or the one listening?
_____

9. a. What does Provine call laughter? Use his exact words to complete this statement: Provine calls laughter "_____."
   b. What does this mean? Use your own words. _____
_____

Discussion

Work with a partner. Talk about your answers to these questions.

1. How did the researchers carry out the first study described in the reading? Tell what the researchers were interested in, who took part in the study, and what they had to do.

2. According to the reading, the female college students in the study

   a. laughed most with male friends and

   b. laughed in a higher voice with male strangers.

   Why do you think they laughed like this?

3. Research on laughter shows that the average adult laughs about seventeen times a day. How many times do you think you laugh during the day? What kinds of things make you laugh?

4. What do you think is the difference between "laughing at someone" and "laughing with someone"?

Using New Words

Work with a partner. Choose five target words or phrases from the chart on page 204. On a piece of paper, use each word or phrase in a sentence.

Writing

Choose a topic. Write a paragraph.

1. Some people say, "Laughter is the best medicine." Do you agree? Why or why not?

2. "Laugh and the world laughs with you" is a common saying in English. Think of a common saying about laughter in your first language. Tell what it is, what it means, and why you do or don't agree with it.

CHAPTER 19

The Inventor of the Telephone

The inventor of the telephone

GETTING READY TO READ

Mark your answers to the following questions. Then discuss your answers in a small group or with the whole class.

1. Who invented the telephone?

☐ Thomas Edison ☐ Guglielmo Marconi ☐ Alexander Graham Bell

2. How many times a day do you usually use a phone?

☐ 0–2 times ☐ 3–10 times ☐ more than 10 times

3. Which of the following communication tools do you use regularly?

☐ a telephone with a landline ☐ a pay phone ☐ a cell phone

☐ other: _____

Look at the pictures, words, and definitions next to the reading. Then read without stopping.

The Inventor of the Telephone

1   If you cannot imagine how you would **get along** without your phone, then say a word of thanks to its inventor, Alexander Graham Bell. Bell was born in Scotland in 1847. All through his life, he had a strong interest in communication, **partly** because of the influence of his family. His grandfather was an actor and a famous **speech** teacher, and his father developed the first international phonetic alphabet.[1] His mother's influence was rather different. Communication took a great **effort** for her because she was almost completely **deaf**. She usually held a tube[2] to her ear **in order to** hear people. Her son Alexander discovered another way to communicate with her when he was a little boy. He used to **press** his mouth against her forehead[3] and speak in a low voice. The sound waves traveled to her ears through the bones of her head. This was among the first of his many discoveries about sound.

2   As a teenager, Bell taught music and public speaking at a boys' school. In his free time, he had fun working on **various** inventions with an older brother, inventions that included a useful machine for farmwork. Then both of Bell's brothers got sick and died. He **came down with** the same terrible sickness—tuberculosis[4]—leading his parents to move the family to Canada. There his health returned.

3   Bell moved to the United States when he was twenty-four. He went to Boston to teach at a school for deaf children. In Boston, he fell in love with Mabel Hubbard, a student of his who later became his wife. During this period of his life, Bell was a very busy man. **In addition to** teaching, he was working on several inventions.

4   Bell's main goal was to make machines to help deaf people hear. He was also trying to improve on[5] the telegraph.[6] In those days, the telegraph was the only way to send information quickly over a long distance. Telegraph messages traveled over

[1] a *phonetic alphabet* = a way to show the sounds of words, for example *laugh* = /læf/ or /läf/

[2] a hearing *tube*

[3] *forehead*

[4] *tuberculosis* = a serious sickness that affects a person's ability to breathe

[5] *improve on* = make something better than

[6] a *telegraph* operator sending a message

wires and were sent in Morse code,[7] which used long and short sounds for the letters of the alphabet. Bell was trying to find a way to send the human voice along a wire. However, almost no one believed in this idea, and people kept telling him, "You're **wasting** your time. You should try to invent a better telegraph—that's where the money is."

5   Bell understood a great deal about sound and electricity, but he was actually not very good at building things. Luckily, he met someone who was, a man named Thomas Watson, who turned out to be a great help to Bell. One day—it was March 10, 1876—the two men were working in **separate** rooms. They were getting ready to test a new invention, which had a wire going from one room to the other. Something **went wrong** and Bell **shouted**, "Mr. Watson, come here. I want you!" His voice traveled along the wire, and Watson heard it coming from the new machine. It was the world's first telephone call. Bell may or may not have realized it at the time, but he was on his way to becoming a very rich man.

6   Soon afterward, Bell wrote to his father:

> The day is coming when telegraph wires will [go] to houses just like water or gas—and friends will converse with each other without leaving home.

Maybe his father laughed to hear this idea. At the time, most people expected the phone to be just a tool for business, not something that anyone would ever have at home. Bell could see a greater future for it, but even he could probably never have imagined what telephones are like today.

The quotation from Alexander Graham Bell's letter to his father comes from the April 1999 Library of Congress Information Bulletin. Retrieved March 9, 2009, from http://www.loc.gov/loc/lcib/9904/bell.html.

. . . – – . . .

[7] *Morse code* for SOS, a call for help

Quick Comprehension Check

Read these sentences. Circle T (true) or F (false).

1. Alexander Graham Bell's family influenced his career. T F

2. Bell started inventing things while he was growing up. T F

3. He was born and grew up in the United States. T F

4. He never married. T F

5. He invented the telephone working all alone. T F

6. He believed that in the future, people would have phones at home. T F

EXPLORING VOCABULARY

Thinking about the Target Vocabulary

 Find the three nouns, six verbs, and three adjectives in **bold** in "The Inventor of the Telephone." Add them to the chart. Use the singular form of any plural noun and the base form of each verb.

	Nouns	Verbs	Adjectives	Other
1				
				partly
				in order to
2				
3				in addition to
4				
5				

B Which words are new to you? Circle them in the chart. Then find the words in the reading. Look at the context. Can you guess the meaning?

Using the Target Vocabulary

A These sentences are **about the reading**. Complete them with the words and phrases in the box.

deaf	in addition to	partly	speech	waste
get along	in order to	separate	various	went wrong

1. Some people could not manage to live very well without a telephone. They could not _____ without one.
2. Some, but not all, of Bell's interest in communication was because of his family. It came _____ from their influence on him.
3. Bell's grandfather taught people to speak well. He was a _____ teacher.
4. Bell's mother could hear only a little. She was almost completely _____.
5. She used a tube _____ hear people. She used it for this purpose.
6. As a teenager, Bell worked with his brother on _____ inventions. They built a variety of things together.
7. Bell had a teaching job in Boston. He also had more to do. _____ his job, he worked on several inventions.
8. People told Bell to use his time carefully. They told him not to _____ his time.
9. On March 10, 1876, Bell and his partner were not working in the same room. They were in _____ rooms.
10. While he was working, Bell had an accident of some kind. Something _____.

These sentences use the target words and phrases **in new contexts**. Complete them with the words and phrases in the box.

deaf	go wrong	in order to	separate	various
get along	in addition to	partly	speech	waste

1. The sky was only _____ cloudy in the morning but completely cloudy later on.
2. I have to shout in order for him to hear me. He's getting

   _____.
3. This type of car is available in _____ colors.
4. Only human beings can express themselves through

   _____.
5. I keep my notes for each of my courses in _____ parts of my notebook.
6. You don't really need a car in this city. You can _____ using buses and the subway.
7. Relax! I'm sure everything will go smoothly. Nothing will

   _____.
8. Don't _____ your money on that movie. We saw it, and it was very disappointing.
9. He took science courses _____ prepare for a career in medicine.
10. We use laughter to communicate, _____ words and other sounds.

Read each definition and look at the paragraph number. Look back at the reading on pages 212–213 to find the **boldfaced** word or phrase to match the definition. Copy it in the chart.

Definition	Paragraph	Target Word or Phrase
1. the energy (of mind or body) needed to do something	1	
2. push something against something else	1	
3. started to have (a sickness)	2	
4. long, thin pieces of metal, like threads, used for carrying electricity or sound waves	4	
5. said something in a very loud voice	5	

Building on the Vocabulary: Studying Collocations

Remember: Certain verbs go with certain nouns. Use the verbs *make*, *take*, and *put* with the noun *effort*. Also note that *effort* is sometimes a count noun and sometimes a noncount noun. Study these examples:

- make an effort to do something
- it takes (an/some) effort to do something
- put (some/a lot of) effort into something

A Complete the sentences. Use *make*, *put*, or *take*.

1. Does it _____ a lot of effort to learn a language?
2. Please _____ an effort to be on time.
3. He won't _____ any effort into his homework.

B On a piece of paper, write three sentences with *make*, *put*, and *take* + *effort*.

DEVELOPING YOUR SKILLS

Reading Between the Lines

Are the following statements true or false? You cannot scan the reading for the answers. You must think about what the reading says and decide. Circle T or F, and give one or more reasons for your answer. Write complete sentences.

1. Alexander Graham Bell was probably close to his family.　　(T)　F

His family influenced his career, and he and his brother invented
things together.

2. Tuberculosis was a more serious sickness in the 1800s
than now.　　　　　　　　　　　　　　　　　　　　　T　F

_____

_____

3. Bell's wife was deaf.　　　　　　　　　　　　　　T　F

_____

_____

4. What Bell wanted most in life was to become rich and famous.　T　F

_____

_____

5. Thomas Watson believed in Bell's ideas when others did not.　T　F

_____

_____

Text Organization

Look back at the reading "The Inventor of the Telephone." How is the information in the reading organized? Check (✓) your answer.

☐ **1.** Each paragraph compares one thing with another.

☐ **2.** The paragraphs are all about causes and effects.

☐ **3.** The paragraphs are in chronological order (time order).

Summarizing

On a piece of paper, write a summary of "The Inventor of the Telephone." Use no more than ten sentences. Use your own words. That is, do not copy sentences from the reading. Include:

- the inventor's name
- why he is famous
- when and where he was born
- where he spent his life
- his main goal as an inventor
- the date of the first phone call

Discussion

Talk about these questions in a small group.

1. How did Alexander Graham Bell's family influence his career?

2. Have you ever spent one or more days in a place where you had no phone nearby? If so, where were you? Describe your feelings about being far from a phone.

3. Imagine the perfect telephone of the future. What will it be like? What will it be able to do?

Using New Words

Work with a partner. Choose five target words or phrases from the chart on page 214. On a piece of paper, use each word or phrase in a sentence.

Writing

Choose a topic. Write a paragraph.

1. How important are telephones in your life? Why and how often do you make or get phone calls? Write about your relationship with the telephone.

2. Complete this sentence: I wish somebody would invent . . . Explain why this invention would be a good thing.

Chapter 20 header

CHAPTER 20 — Speaking with Your Eyes

Making eye contact

GETTING READY TO READ

Answer the questions with a partner or in a small group. Then talk about your answers with the class.

1. How do you communicate with other people? Make a list of the ways.

2. Do you know the phrase *nonverbal communication*? It refers to communication that happens without words. Give examples of how you can say something:

   by using your face

   by using your hands

   with the way you stand or move

3. How can you read people by looking at those same things? What kinds of things do you notice? What do they mean?

READING

Look at the picture, words, and definitions next to the reading. Then read without stopping.

Speaking with Your Eyes

1 When we think about communicating with other people, we usually think about talking or writing. That is, we think about using words. However, much of the communication that takes place **in person** happens without words. It happens through nonverbal communication. We send nonverbal messages in many ways, **including** with our face, our hands, and the ways we stand, move, and use the **space** around us. We get messages from others in the same ways. Our eyes play an especially important role. Researchers who study this role use the **term** *eye behavior*. It refers to both the things we do with our eyes without realizing it and the things we do **on purpose**.

2 One area of eye behavior is eye contact.[1] Imagine yourself walking along a busy city sidewalk.[2] What are your eyes doing? Do you focus on anything, or are your eyes moving all the time? What are other people's eyes doing? If you are in a U.S. city, there are probably few people making eye contact. If your eyes meet a stranger's, **chances are** that he or she will quickly look away. If the stranger does not look away but **maintains** eye contact, then that may be a **sign** of **attraction**.

3 We often use our eyes to express interest in someone. Eye contact shows that we are paying attention. It may be **merely** an effort to be polite, or it may mean something more. Because it is natural to look at things we find attractive, keeping our eyes on someone can be like paying the person a compliment.[3]

4 Looking at something attractive actually **brings about** a change in our eyes. It makes our pupils—those small **round** black areas in the middle of our eyes—grow larger. Large pupils then make our eyes more attractive.

5 Research has shown that eye contact influences whether someone finds another person attractive. In a study at the University of Aberdeen, Dr. Claire Conway asked participants[4]

(continued)

[1] *eye contact* = two people looking at each other's eyes at the same time

[2] a *sidewalk*

[3] *pay someone a compliment* = say something nice about someone

[4] a *participant* = someone who is taking part in an activity or event

to look at photos of faces. There were photos of people smiling and looking **directly** at the viewer,[5] and there were photos of those same people smiling but looking away. Dr. Conway said, "Faces that were looking directly at the viewer were **judged** more attractive." This was especially true for faces of the opposite sex. Dr. Conway suggests that something in the human brain makes us prefer the faces of people who make eye contact with us. When they are looking at us, they seem to like us. If they like us, that makes them more attractive to us.

[5] a *viewer* = a person who is looking or watching

6   Of course, a face in a photo is one thing, and a real person looking at you is something else. How do you feel when someone makes eye contact with you and keeps on looking? Does it make the person seem attractive, or does it make you feel uncomfortable, or even afraid?

7   How we read people's eye behavior depends in part on our culture. In some cultures, making and keeping eye contact shows respect. In others, it has the opposite effect. As we grow up, we learn the rules of our culture for nonverbal communication in general and eye contact in particular.[6] We learn what we are expected to do and what we are **allowed** to do. But even as an adult, you may find there is still more to learn about the language of the eyes.

[6] *in particular* = especially or specifically

Dr. Conway was quoted in "Direct gaze makes you more attractive." Retrieved March 9, 2009, from http://www.physorg.com/news113664580.html.

Quick Comprehension Check

Read these sentences. Circle T (true) or F (false).

1. *Nonverbal communication* means communication without words.   T   F

2. How you use your eyes is part of nonverbal communication.   T   F

3. *Making eye contact* means looking at someone else's eyes.   T   F

4. Most eye contact happens by accident.   T   F

5. Eye contact can mean "I like you."   T   F

6. Eye behavior is the same across cultures.   T   F

EXPLORING VOCABULARY

Thinking about the Target Vocabulary

 Find the four nouns, four verbs, and one adjective in **bold** in "Speaking with Your Eyes." Add them to the chart. Use the singular form of any plural noun and the base form of each verb.

	Nouns	Verbs	Adjectives	Other
1				in person
				including
				on purpose
2				chances are
3				merely
4				
5				directly
7				

B Which words are new to you? Circle them in the chart. Then find the words in the reading. Look at the context. Can you guess the meaning?

Using the Target Vocabulary

 These sentences are about the reading. What is the meaning of each boldfaced word or phrase? Circle a, b, or c.

1. You can talk to someone either **in person** or on the phone. *In person* means
   a. in someone's ear.   **b.** in the same place   **c.** by shouting at
                          as someone else.   someone.

2. The **term** *eye behavior* refers to what our eyes do. A term is
   a. a word or phrase.   **b.** a study.   **c.** an explanation.

3. You can control your eyes and look at someone **on purpose**. *On purpose* means
   a. by accident.   **b.** in a planned way.   **c.** partly.

4. Sometimes people make eye contact and **maintain** it. *Maintain something* means
   a. make it continue.   **b.** waste it.   **c.** prefer it.

5. Looking someone in the eye can show **attraction**. *Attraction* means
   a. a readiness to fight.   **b.** a sense of being   **c.** a strong feeling of
                              bored.   liking.

6. Looking at something or someone you like **brings about** a change in your eyes. *Bring something about* means
   a. notice it.   **b.** destroy it.   **c.** cause it.

7. The pupils of your eyes are **round**. *Round* means
   a. easy to pronounce.   **b.** strong and   **c.** shaped like a
                            powerful.   circle or a ball.

8. People in the study preferred faces that were looking **directly** at them. *Directly* means
   a. sharply.   **b.** exactly.   **c.** unfortunately.

9. People in the study looked at faces and **judged** which ones were more attractive. *To judge something* means
   a. to search for it   **b.** to get along   **c.** to form and give an
                          without it.   opinion about it.

10. Cultural rules tell us what we can do and what we are not **allowed** to do. If you allow people to do something, you

    a. realize that they   **b.** explain how to   **c.** let them do it.
       are doing it.   do it.

B   These sentences use the target words and phrases **in new contexts.** Complete them with the words and phrases in the box.

allowed	bring about	in person	maintaining	round
attraction	directly	judging	on purpose	terms

1. The owner of the café set some small _____ tables out on the sidewalk.

2. In the game of soccer, only the goalkeeper is _____ to touch the ball with his or her hands.

3. _____ by their laughter, I'd guess that they're having a good time.

4. The boy felt bad about breaking his little sister's toy. He didn't do it _____.

5. The bank is _____ across the street from the post office.

6. I didn't understand some of the _____ the professor used in her lecture.

7. You can apply for the job online or go to the office and apply _____.

8. The company works hard at _____ good relationships with their customers.

9. The greatest presidents _____ the most important political changes.

10. The man was so boring that Carol's friends couldn't understand her _____ to him.

Read these sentences. Write the boldfaced target words and phrases next to their definitions.

a. Those birds are a **sign** that winter is ending and spring is coming.

b. Jack hates riding on crowded trains. He needs a lot of personal **space**.

c. There was no need to get upset. She was **merely** making a joke.

d. There were four couples at John's birthday dinner, **including** John and his wife.

e. If you review your notes for the test, **chances are** you'll do well on it.

Target Words and Phrases	Definitions
1. _____	= the empty area between people or things
2. _____	= an event or fact that shows that something is happening
3. _____	= it is probably true that
4. _____	= having something as a part (of a larger group)
5. _____	= just, only (showing that something is not especially important)

Building on the Vocabulary: Word Grammar

The verbs *allow* and *let* have the same meaning but are used differently in sentences.

allow:

- Use *allow* + someone + *to* + verb: Please **allow my son to leave** school at 1:30 today.
- Use *be* + *allowed to* + verb: You **aren't allowed to park** there.
- Use *allow* + noun (or verb + *-ing*): Do they **allow pets**? Do they **allow smoking**?

let:

- Use *let* + someone + verb: Please **let my son leave** school at 1:30 today.

A Complete the sentences. Use *allow* or *let*.

1. My parents wouldn't _____ me have a dog.
2. The high school doesn't _____ students to park in that lot.
3. _____ the other car go first.
4. Will the teacher _____ dictionaries during the test?
5. The town does not _____ fishing at the public beach.

B On a piece of paper, write two sentences. Use *allow* and *let*.

DEVELOPING YOUR SKILLS

Defining Terms

Use information from the reading to define these terms.

1. nonverbal communication _____

_____

2. eye behavior _____

_____

3. making eye contact _____

_____

Cause and Effect

Use information from the reading to complete the diagram.

Cause		Effect
1.	→	the pupils of your eyes grow larger
2. the pupils of your eyes grow larger	→	
3. a face in a photo is smiling and looking right at you	→	
4. someone makes and maintains eye contact		Possible positive effects:
	→	Possible negative effects:

Fact vs. Opinion

 A Decide if each statement expresses a fact or an opinion. Base your answers on information from the reading. Circle Fact or Opinion.

1. Researchers study eye behavior in nonverbal communication.   Fact / Opinion

2. Making eye contact is one type of eye behavior.   Fact / Opinion

3. People naturally look at things they find attractive.   Fact / Opinion

4. It is a bad idea to make eye contact with strangers.   Fact / Opinion

5. Your culture influences your eye behavior.   Fact / Opinion

6. You should look people in the eye to show respect.   Fact / Opinion

B Write two sentences.

1. Write a fact about eye behavior. _____

_____

2. Write an opinion of your own about eye behavior. _____

_____

Discussion

Talk about these questions in a small group or with your class.

1. According to the reading, what eye behavior would you expect of people walking along a busy city sidewalk in the United States? Would it be the same or different on a street in your hometown? Explain.

2. According to the reading, what can eye contact communicate?

3. How do people use eye behavior to show respect in your culture?

4. What effect do you think wearing sunglasses has on a person's eye behavior? What effect may his or her sunglasses have on other people? Why?

Using New Words

Work with a partner. Choose five target words or phrases from the chart on page 223. On a piece of paper, use each word or phrase in a sentence.

Writing

Choose a topic. Write a paragraph.

1. When is it important to make eye contact? Give some advice for making eye contact and using other kinds of nonverbal communication.

2. There are many well-known sayings about eyes in English, such as "The eyes are the window to the soul," meaning that you can understand what is in a person's mind and heart by looking into his or her eyes. Give a saying about eyes from your first language, explain what it means, and give your opinion about it.

Wrap-up

REVIEWING VOCABULARY

 A **Match the words in the box with their definitions. There are four extra words.**

actually	deaf	merely	role	speech	voice
allow	male	prefer	sense	stranger	warn

1. _____ = unable to hear

2. _____ = really and truly (even though it may surprise you)

3. _____ = the ability to speak or the way someone speaks

4. _____ = the sound someone makes when singing or speaking

5. _____ = know or feel something without seeing or being told about it

6. _____ = like or want (some person or thing) more than another

7. _____ = the job, position, or function that someone or something has

8. _____ = tell someone that something bad or dangerous may happen

B Complete the sentences with words or phrases from the box. There are two extra words or phrases.

bring about	coming down with	in addition to	in other words
carrying out	get along	including	in person
chances are	go wrong	in order to	on purpose

1. I think I'm _____ a cold.

2. It took years of effort to _____ a change in the law.

3. If you try to call her before 10:00 A.M., _____ she'll still be asleep.

4. I had to take two buses _____ get there.

5. Somehow he manages to do a weekend job _____ his regular job.

6. He claims it was an accident, but I think he did it

   _____.

7. I really need my car. I couldn't _____ without it.

8. The bill comes to $19.95, _____ the tax.

9. You can apply by mail, but it's faster to do it _____.

10. Have you thought about what to do if things _____?

EXPANDING VOCABULARY

Complete the chart of word families with **boldfaced** words from the sentences below.

	Nouns	Verbs	Adjectives	Adverbs
1.	attraction	attract	attractive	attractively
2.				
3.				
4.				
5.				

1. **a.** Flowers **attract** certain insects, like bees.
   b. She is an **attractive** young woman.
   c. She is always **attractively** dressed.
   d. It was easy to see the **attraction** between Jack and Diana.

2. **a.** It was just a friendly **competition**.
   b. Their products are **competitively** priced.
   c. He and his brother are highly **competitive**.
   d. I give up! I can't **compete** with you.

3. **a.** That actor has very **expressive** eyes.
   b. Did you see the **expression** on her face when she got the news?
   c. It's hard for me to **express** myself.
   d. He sings so **expressively**!

4. **a.** Do boys and girls go to **separate** schools in your country?
   b. They arrived at the party **separately** but left together.
   c. **Separate** the light-colored clothes from the dark ones before washing them.
   d. They were married for five years before their **separation**.

5. **a.** Don't **waste** water.
   b. Taxpayers get angry if the government spends **wastefully**.
   c. What a **waste** of time!
   d. He'll have to change his **wasteful** spending habits.

A PUZZLE

Complete the sentences with words you studied in Chapters 17–20. Write the words in the puzzle.

Across

1. Her strange _____ worried her friends.

6. The sound of _____ filled the room.

7. The shortest distance between two points is a _____ line.

9. There was no _____ of emotion on his face.

11. He has many friends and a busy _____ life.

12. He got the job _____ his own efforts, not because of family connections.

Down

2. Please make an _____ to be on time.

3. I have socks in _____ colors.

4. Before you leave the plane, check for your _____ belongings.

5. It's too early to _____ whether the plan is a success.

8. The letter "O" is _____.

10. _____ winds drove the forest fire across the region.

BUILDING DICTIONARY SKILLS

 A **Words often have more than one meaning. Look at this entry for** *direction*. **Write the number of the meaning used in each sentence below.**

_____ **1.** Read the **directions** before you start the test.

_____ **2.** A *one-way street* means traffic goes in one **direction** only.

_____ **3.** His life is taking a new **direction**.

_____ **4.** He has a good sense of **direction**, but he always takes a map, too.

_____ **5.** The company has grown under McCrae's **direction**.

> di•rec•tion /dəˈrɛkʃən, daɪ-/ *n*
> **1** [C] the way someone or something is moving, facing, or aimed: *Brian drove off* **in the direction of** (=toward) *the party.* | *As she walked along the trail, she saw a large man coming in* **the opposite direction**. **2** [C] the general way in which someone or something changes or develops: *Suddenly the conversation changed direction.* **3 directions** [plural] instructions about how to go from one place to another, or about how to do something: *Could you* **give me directions to** *the airport?* | *Read the directions at the top of the page.* **4** [U] control, guidance, or advice: *The company's been successful* **under** *Martini's* **direction**. **5** [U] a general purpose or aim: *Sometimes I feel that my life lacks direction.* **6 sense of direction** the ability to know which way to go in a place you do not know well

B **Look at this entry for the noun** *wave*. **Write the number of the meaning used in each sentence below.**

_____ **1.** The child gave her mother a **wave** and ran to join her friends.

_____ **2.** The **waves** are too big for people to swim today.

_____ **3.** When I heard the news, I felt a **wave** of fear come over me.

_____ **4.** Light and sound move in **waves**.

> wave[1] /weɪv/ *n* [C] **1** an area of raised water that moves across the surface of the ocean or another large area of water: *waves breaking on the beach* **2** a sudden increase in a particular emotion, activity, number, etc.: *a recent* **crime wave** | *a* **wave of** *nostalgia for his childhood* | *a sudden wave of nausea* | *a* **great wave** *of immigrants from Eastern Europe* **3** the movement you make when you wave your hand: *She left with* **a wave of** *her* **hand**. **4** a part of your hair that curls slightly: *a wave in her hair* **5** the form in which some types of energy move: *light/sound/radio waves* **6 make waves** *informal* to cause problems: *We have a job to finish, so don't make waves, OK?* ®HEATWAVE

Vocabulary Self-Test 3

Circle the letter of the word or phrase that best completes each sentence.

Example:

Thousands of people were in the streets to _____ in the celebration.

a. explain   **b.** pick up   **c.** take part   **d.** discover

1. Long-_____ phone calls used to be very expensive.

   a. root   **b.** distance   **c.** magic   **d.** score

2. Tim asked me for advice, and I _____ that he call you instead.

   a. competed   **b.** afforded   **c.** suggested   **d.** joined

3. The books were so _____ that it was clear no one had touched them in a long while.

   a. kind   **b.** dusty   **c.** popular   **d.** female

4. There were no problems. Everything went _____.

   a. partly   **b.** rather   **c.** yet   **d.** smoothly

5. As you walk down Main Street _____ City Hall, you'll see the library on your left.

   a. forward   **b.** in order to   **c.** toward   **d.** nearly

6. Paul _____ that he can tell what I'm thinking by the look on my face.

   a. claims   **b.** wastes   **c.** melts   **d.** matters

7. I've seen him do some dangerous things. That man has no _____!

   a. basis   **b.** behavior   **c.** fear   **d.** level

8. I saw only the front page of the newspaper, but Lora read the
   _____ thing.
   a. professional   **b.** specific   **c.** low   **d.** entire

9. Of course she's upset. _____, you promised to help her, and
   now you say you can't.
   a. No longer   **b.** After all   **c.** No matter   **d.** Whenever

10. We'll have to finish talking about this later. The meeting
    _____ to start.
    a. is about   **b.** comes out   **c.** goes on   **d.** in addition

11. The more energy a sound _____ has, the louder the sound.
    a. wire   **b.** amount   **c.** wave   **d.** weight

12. This weekend, we'll have to _____ our clocks back one hour.
    a. concern   **b.** set   **c.** share   **d.** attract

13. He's shorter _____ than he looks on TV.
    a. in person   **b.** right away   **c.** on purpose   **d.** except

14. Mary had to close down her business. I don't know what
    _____.
    a. went wrong   **b.** got along   **c.** worked out   **d.** made up

15. The researchers _____ a study on how chocolate affects the
    brain.
    a. turned into   **b.** came down   **c.** sensed   **d.** carried out
                            with

16. Henry has never given a speech before. _____ he's nervous.
    a. Anymore   **b.** No doubt   **c.** Immediately   **d.** Including

17. Dr. Hernandez has had a fifty-two-year _____ in medicine.
    a. purpose   **b.** shock   **c.** career   **d.** stranger

18. The cat lay very _____ while watching the bird.
    a. powerful   **b.** clearly   **c.** round   **d.** still

19. The house is 200 _____ years old.
    a. or so   **b.** all of a sudden **c.** outdoors   **d.** daily

20. David _____ to leave work early without the boss knowing.

    a. warned   **b.** managed   **c.** noticed   **d.** advanced

21. Did you _____ good eye contact during your interview?

    a. hide   **b.** express   **c.** support   **d.** maintain

22. The sick man didn't try to speak. It was too much of an _____.

    a. attraction   **b.** opportunity   **c.** increase   **d.** effort

23. There was a foot of snow on the _____.

    a. study   **b.** ground   **c.** choice   **d.** period

24. Let's wait to see the _____ of the new law.

    a. space   **b.** term   **c.** effect   **d.** variety

25. The boy doesn't mean to hurt the other children, but he doesn't _____ how strong he is.

    a. realize   **b.** lead   **c.** prefer   **d.** develop

26. I thought her name was Joan, but it's _____ JoAnne.

    a. according to   **b.** however   **c.** naturally   **d.** actually

27. I thought he would be angry, but he _____ laughed.

    a. in general   **b.** directly   **c.** merely   **d.** highly

28. We couldn't find two seats together on the train, so we sat in _____ places.

    a. social   **b.** bright   **c.** separate   **d.** brave

29. The company will offer more training at _____ times during the next year.

    a. straight   **b.** weak   **c.** sharp   **d.** various

30. Changes in class size will _____ all teachers and students.

    a. affect   **b.** quit   **c.** judge   **d.** escape

31. The tax increase will not _____ to anyone who makes less than $25,000 a year.

    a. apply   **b.** contain   **c.** review   **d.** feed

32. After a great deal of hard work, he _____ his goal.

    a. turned out   **b.** reached   **c.** prepared   **d.** rushed

33. You can _____ the results of your test tomorrow.

    a. disappear   **b.** encourage   **c.** expect   **d.** stare

34. Nancy is lonely. She has no friends _____.

    a. at all   **b.** alike   **c.** through   **d.** activity

35. _____ Dan has the right tools for the job, he really doesn't have the skills.

    a. Somehow   **b.** Chances are   **c.** Once   **d.** Although

36. We were glad to see _____ that Mom is finally feeling better.

    a. memories   **b.** directions   **c.** signs   **d.** speech

37. I _____ understood anything he said. What about you?

    a. hardly   **b.** difficulty   **c.** politely   **d.** first of all

38. The prison _____ visitors only on weekends.

    a. presses   **b.** allows   **c.** divides   **d.** creates

39. I can hear you perfectly well. You don't have to _____.

    a. deaf   **b.** shout   **c.** voice   **d.** pronounce

40. _____ you review your notes for the next test.

    a. Get over   **b.** Bring about   **c.** Get into   **d.** Make sure

See the Answer Key on page 240.

Vocabulary Self-Tests Answer Key

Below are the answers to the Vocabulary Self-Tests. Check your answers, and then review any words you did not remember. You can look up a word in the Index to Target Vocabulary on pages 241–243. Then go back to the reading and exercises to find the word. Use your dictionary as needed.

Vocabulary Self-Test 1, Units 1–2 (pages 91–93)

1. d. gets to
2. a. choice
3. a. no doubt
4. c. boring
5. d. reach
6. b. hide
7. a. specific
8. d. danger
9. b. weigh
10. a. yet
11. b. figure out
12. d. cultures
13. c. opposite
14. a. mentioned
15. a. average
16. a. areas
17. b. Although
18. d. deal with
19. c. control
20. b. talent
21. d. power
22. a. hardly
23. b. is about to
24. c. difference
25. a. cover
26. b. nearly
27. c. aware
28. d. kind

Vocabulary Self-Test 2, Units 3–4 (pages 186–188)

1. b. amounts
2. c. search
3. a. exactly
4. d. That is
5. a. destroyed
6. d. make up
7. b. producer
8. c. record
9. d. Unfortunately
10. a. comes up
11. d. programs
12. b. certain
13. c. available
14. a. focus
15. c. rate
16. a. no matter
17. d. do
18. b. emotions
19. b. calm
20. a. supplies
21. c. communication
22. d. medicine
23. c. gentle
24. b. insect
25. c. closet
26. a. series
27. b. mean
28. b. According to
29. d. up to
30. c. notes

Vocabulary Self-Test 3, Units 1–5 (pages 235–238)

1. b. distance
2. c. suggested
3. b. dusty
4. d. smoothly
5. c. toward
6. a. claims
7. c. fear
8. d. entire
9. b. After all
10. a. is about
11. c. wave
12. b. set
13. a. in person
14. a. went wrong

15. d. carried out
16. b. No doubt
17. c. career
18. d. still
19. a. or so
20. b. managed
21. d. maintain
22. d. effort
23. b. ground
24. c. effect
25. a. realize
26. d. actually
27. c. merely
28. c. separate

29. d. various
30. a. affect
31. a. apply
32. b. reached
33. c. expect
34. a. at all
35. d. Although
36. c. signs
37. a. hardly
38. b. allows
39. b. shout
40. d. Make sure

INDEX TO TARGET VOCABULARY